1895

WITHDRAWN

India in the West

The Asian American Experience

THE ASIAN AMERICAN EXPERIENCE

India in the West

SOUTH ASIANS IN AMERICA

Ronald Takaki

PROFESSOR OF ETHNIC STUDIES
AT THE UNIVERSITY OF CALIFORNIA, BERKELEY

Adapted by Rebecca Stefoff

WITH CAROL TAKAKI

Chelsea House Publishers

New York Philadelphia

On the cover An Indian family photographed shortly before their arrival in America in the 1960s.

Chelsea House Publishers

EDITORIAL DIRECTOR   Richard Rennert
EXECUTIVE MANAGING EDITOR   Karyn Gullen Browne
COPY CHIEF   Robin James
PICTURE EDITOR   Adrian G. Allen
ART DIRECTOR   Robert Mitchell
MANUFACTURING DIRECTOR   Gerald Levine
ASSISTANT ART DIRECTOR   Joan Ferrigno

The Asian American Experience

SENIOR EDITOR   Jake Goldberg
SERIES DESIGN   Marjorie Zaum

Staff for *India in the West*
EDITORIAL ASSISTANT   Scott D. Briggs
PICTURE RESEARCHER   Sandy Jones

Adapted and reprinted from *Strangers from a Different Shore,*
© 1989 by Ronald Takaki, by arrangement with the author
and Little, Brown and Company, Inc.

Text © 1995 by Ronald Takaki. All rights reserved.
Printed and bound in the United States of America.

First Printing

1 3 5 7 9 8 6 4 2

Library of Congress Cataloging-in-Publication Data
Takaki, Ronald T., 1939–
India in the West: South Asians in America/Ronald Takaki.
  p. cm. — (The Asian American Experience)
  Includes bibliographical references and index.
ISBN 0-7910-2186-6
ISBN 0-7910-2193-9
 I. South Asians—North America. I. Title. II. Series: Asian American
Experience (New York, N. Y.)
E49.2.S69T35 1995 94–16885
970.004914—dc20 CIP

Contents

A family in India. The Asian Indian immigrants had a strong sense of obligation to members of their close-knit families and village communities.

From a Different Shore

AS A CHILD IN HAWAII, I GREW UP IN A MULTICULTURAL corner of America. My own family had roots in Japan and China.

Grandfather Kasuke Okawa arrived in Hawaii in 1866, and my father, Toshio Takaki, came as a 13-year-old boy in 1918. My stepfather, Koon Keu Young, sailed from China to the islands when he was a teenager.

My neighbors were Japanese, Chinese, Hawaiian, Filipino, Portuguese, and Korean. Behind my house, Alice Liu and her friends played the traditional Chinese game of mah-jongg late into the night, the clicking of the tiles lulling me to sleep.

Next to us the Miuras flew billowing and colorful carp kites on Japanese boy's day. I heard voices with different accents, different languages, and saw children of different colors.

Together we went barefoot to school and played games like baseball and *jan ken po*. We spoke "pidgin English," a melodious language of the streets and community. "Hey, da kind tako ono, you know," we would say, combining English, Japanese, and Hawaiian. "This octopus is delicious." Racially and culturally diverse, we all thought of ourselves as Americans.

But we did not know why families representing such an array of nationalities from different shores were living together and sharing their cultures and a common language. Our teachers and textbooks did not explain the diversity of our community or the sources of our unity.

7

After graduation from high school, I attended a college in a midwestern town where I found myself invited to "dinners for foreign students" sponsored by local churches and clubs like the Rotary. I politely tried to explain to my kind hosts that I was not a "foreign student." My fellow students and even my professors would ask me how long I had been in America and where I had learned to speak English. "In this country," I would reply. And sometimes I would add: "I was born in America, and my family has been here for three generations."

Asian Americans have been here for over 150 years. They are diverse, coming originally from countries such as China, Japan, Korea, the Philippines, India, Vietnam, Laos, and Cambodia. Many of them live in Chinatowns, the colorful streets filled with sidewalk vegetable stands and crowds of people carrying shopping bags; their communities are also called Little Tokyo, Koreatown, and Little Saigon. Asian Americans work in hot kitchens and bus tables in restaurants with elegant names like Jade Pagoda and Bombay Spice. In garment factories, Chinese and Korean women hunch over whirling sewing machines, their babies sleeping nearby on blankets. In the Silicon Valley of California, rows and rows of Vietnamese and Laotian women serve as the eyes and hands of production assembly lines for computer chip industries. Tough Chinese gang members strut on Grant Avenue in San Francisco and Canal Street in New York's Chinatown. In La Crosse, Wisconsin, Hmong refugees from Laos, now dependent on welfare, sit and stare at the snowdrifts outside their windows. Asian American engineers do complex research in the laboratories of the high-technology industries along

Route 128 in Massachusetts. Asian Americans seem to be everywhere on university campuses.

Today, Asian Americans belong to the fastest growing ethnic group in the United States. Kept out of the United States by immigration restriction laws in the 19th and early 20th centuries, Asians have recently been coming again to America. The 1965 immigration act reopened the gates to immigrants from Asia, allowing 20,000 immigrants from each country to enter every year. In the early 1990s, half of all immigrants entering annually are Asian.

The growth of the Asian American population has been dramatic: In 1960, there were only 877,934 Asians in the United States, representing a mere one half of 1% of the American people. Thirty years later, they numbered about seven million, or 3% of the population. They included 1,645,000 Chinese, 1,400,000 Filipinos, 845,000 Japanese, 815,000 Asian Indians, 800,000 Koreans, 614,000 Vietnamese, 150,000 Laotians, 147,000 Cambodians, and 90,000 Hmong. By the year 2000, Asian Americans will probably represent 4% of the total United States population. In California, Asian Americans already make up 10% of the state's inhabitants, compared with 7.5% for African Americans.

Yet very little is known about Asian Americans and their history. Many existing history books give Asian Americans only passing notice—or overlook them entirely. "When one hears Americans tell of the immigrants who built this nation," Congressman Norman Mineta of California observed, "one is often led to believe that all our forebearers came from Europe. When one hears stories about the pioneers going West to shape the land, the Asian immigrant is rarely mentioned."

Indeed, many history books have equated "American" with "white" or "European" in origin. In his prize-winning study, *The Uprooted*, Harvard historian Oscar Handlin presented—to use the book's subtitle—"the Epic Story of the Great Migrations that Made the American People." But Handlin's "epic story" completely left out the "uprooted" from lands across the Pacific Ocean and the "great migrations" from Asia that also helped to make "the American people." As Americans, we have origins in Europe, the Americas, Africa, and also Asia.

We need to include Asians in the history of America. How and why, we ask in this series, were the experiences of these various groups—Chinese, Japanese, Korean, Filipino, Asian Indian, and Southeast Asian—similar to and different from each other? Comparing the experiences of different nationalities can help us see what events were particular to a group and also highlight the experiences they all shared.

Why did Asian immigrants leave everything they knew and loved to come to a strange world so far away? They were "pushed" by hardships in the homelands and "pulled" by demands for their labor in Canada, Brazil, and especially the United States. But what were their own fierce dreams—from the first enterprising Chinese miners of the 1850s in search of "Gold Mountain" to the recent refugees fleeing frantically on helicopters and leaking boats from the ravages of war in Vietnam?

Besides their points of origin, we need to examine the experiences of Asian Americans in different geographical regions, especially Hawaii compared with the mainland. The time of arrival also shaped their lives and communities. About one million people entered the United States between the California gold rush of 1849 and the 1924 immigration act that cut off the flow of peoples from Asian countries. After a break of some 40 years, a second group numbering about four million came between 1965 and 1990. How do we compare the two waves of Asian immigration?

To answer our questions in these volumes, we must study Asian Americans as men and women with minds, wills, and voices. By "voices" we mean their own words and stories as told in their oral histories, conversations, speeches, and songs as well as their own writings—diaries, letters, newspapers, novels, and poems. We need to know the ordinary people.

So much of history has been the story of kings and elites, as if the "little people" were invisible and voiceless. An Asian American told an interviewer: "I am a second-generation Korean American without any achievements in life and I have no education. What is it you want to hear from me? My life is not worth telling to anyone." Similarly, a Chinese immigrant said: "You know, it seems to me there's no use in me telling you all this! I was just a simple worker, a farm worker around here. My story is not going to interest anybody." But others realize they are worthy of attention. "What is it you want to know?" an old Filipino immigrant asked a researcher. "Talk about history. What's that . . . ah, the story of my life . . . and how people lived with each other in my time."

Their stories can enable us to understand Asians as actors in the making of history and as people entitled to dignity. "I hope this survey do a lot of good for Chinese people," a Chinese man told an interviewer from Stanford University in the 1920s. "Make American people realize that Chinese people are humans. I think very few American people really know anything about Chinese." Elderly Asians want the younger generations to know about their experiences. "Our stories should be listened to by many young people," said a 91-year-old retired Japanese plantation laborer. "It's for their sake. We really had a hard time, you know."

The stories of Asian immigrations belong to our country's history. They need to be recorded in our history books, for they reflect the making of America as a nation of immigrants, as a place where men and women came to find a new beginning. At first, many Asian immigrants—probably most of them—saw themselves as sojourners, or temporary migrants. Like many European immigrants such as the Italians and Greeks, they came to America thinking they would be here only a short time. They had left their wives and children behind in their homelands. Their plan was to work here for a few years and then return home with money. But, after their arrival, many found themselves staying. They became settlers instead of remaining sojourners. Bringing their families to their adopted country, they began putting down new roots in America.

But, coming here from Asia, many of America's immigrants found they were not allowed to feel at home in the United States. Even their grandchildren and great-grandchildren still find they are not viewed and accepted as Americans. "We feel that we're a guest in someone else's house," said third generation Ron Wakabayashi, National Director of the Japanese American Citizens League, "that we can never really relax and put our feet on the table."

Behind Wakabayashi's complaint is the question: Why have Asian Americans been considered outsiders? America's immigrants from Pacific shores found they were forced to remain strangers in the new land. Their experiences here were profoundly different from the experiences of European immigrants. Asian immigrants had qualities they could not change or hide—the shape of their eyes, the color of their hair, the complexion of their skin. They were subjected not only to cultural and ethnic prejudice but also to racism. Unlike the Irish and other groups from Europe, Asian immigrants were not treated as individuals but as members of a group with distinctive physical characteristics. Regardless of their personal merits, they sadly discovered, they could not gain acceptance in the larger society.

Unlike European immigrants, Asians were victimized by laws and policies that discriminated on the basis of race. The Chinese Exclusion Act of 1882 barred the Chinese from coming to America because they were Chinese. The National Origins Act of 1924 totally prohibited Japanese immigration.

The laws determined not only who could come to America but also who could become citizens. Decades before Asian immigration began, the United States had already defined the complexion of its citizens: the Naturalization Law of 1790 had specified that naturalized citizenship was to be reserved for "whites." This law remained in effect until 1952. Unlike white ethnic immigrants from countries like Ireland, Asian immigrants were denied citizenship and also the right to vote.

But America also had an opposing tradition and vision, springing from the reality of racial and cultural "diversity." Ours has been, as Walt Whitman celebrated so lyrically, "a teeming Nation of nations" composed of a "vast, surging, hopeful army of workers," a new society where all should be welcomed, "Chinese, Irish, German,—all, all, without exceptions." In the early 20th century, a Japanese immigrant described in poetry a lesson that had been learned by farm laborers of different nationalities—Japanese, Filipino, Mexican, and Asian Indian:

> *People harvesting*
> *Work together unaware*
> *Of racial problems.*

A Filipino immigrant laborer in California expressed a similar hope and understanding. America was, Macario Bulosan told his brother Carlos, "not a land of one race or one class of men" but "a new world" of respect and unconditional opportunities for all who toiled and suffered from oppression, from "the first Indian that offered peace in Manhattan to the last Filipino pea pickers." Asian immigrants came here, as one of them expressed it, searching for "a door into America" and seeking "to build a new life with untried materials." He asked: "Would it be possible for an immigrant like me to become a part of the American dream?"

This series invites students to learn how Asian Americans belong to the larger story of the rich multicultural mosaic called the United States of America.

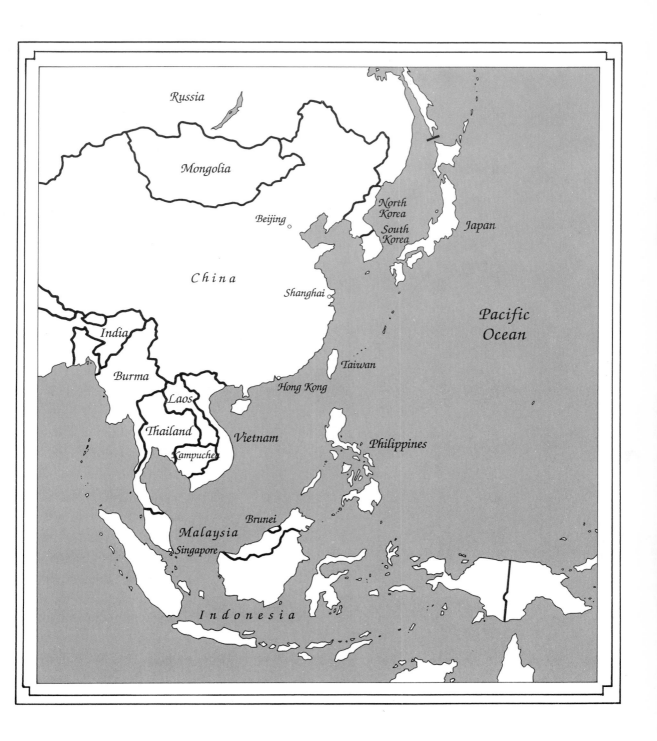

Nearly all of those who streamed into North America from India in the first wave of immigration were men.

SOMETIME IN THE 1880S, A BOY NAMED TULY SINGH JOHL was born in Jundialla, a village in northern India. He was only four years old when two of his older brothers left the village for the sugarcane fields of Australia. They were not alone. In those years, many young men were leaving their homes in India to seek work elsewhere. Tuly grew up in Jundialla, laboring on his family's land. He married when he was about 20 years old, and soon he and his wife had their first child, a boy.

Then, in 1907, Tuly received a letter from his brothers in Australia. It contained money—enough money for Tuly to leave Jundialla, if he wanted to do so. Life was hard in the village. Taxes were going up again, and it was becoming more and more difficult to scrape a living from the land. Tuly had heard about men from villages like his who had emigrated to North America, where there were said to be plenty of jobs. These emigrants had been able to send money home to India to make life easier for their families. Tuly Singh Johl decided to go to Canada and look for work. He would become one of the many immigrants from Asia who powered the railroad, mining, lumber, and farming industries of western North America.

North American employers had been interested in Asian Indian laborers for many years. As early as 1865, the sugarcane planters in Hawaii had thought that India might be a good source of labor for the cane fields and sugar mills. A newspaper called the *Pacific Commercial Advertiser* had asked where the planters would turn to meet the need for workers. The paper gave its own reply: "We answer, to the East Indies. From the teeming millions of Bengal and other provinces of Hindostan." By the mid-1880s, however, immigrants from China and Japan had largely filled the cane planters' labor needs. Nonetheless, the emigration of Asian Indians had begun. A few went to Hawaii; most of them went to Canada and the United States. They came to North America in far smaller numbers than the Chinese and Japanese immigrants who had come before them. But through their work, settlement, and struggle for civil rights, the Asian Indians played an important part in the creation of multicultural America.

The Asian Indians included fewer women than any other group of immigrants from Asia—less than 1% were women. Most of the immigrants were young men, between 16 and 35 years old. Many of them were married, although they did not bring their wives across the sea with them. In 1907, a researcher who interviewed many of the Asian Indian immigrants reported that "practically all" of the newcomers were married and had families in India. Few of the early Asian Indian immigrants were well educated; nearly half of them could neither read nor write. Most of them had been unskilled laborers and agricultural workers in India. Their family and community ties remained strong after they left home; they came to America in small groups of cousins and village neighbors, and these relationships formed a network of interconnections among them in the new country as they lived and worked together.

A large majority of the first immigrants from India were Punjabis, from a region called the Punjab. Known as the "land of five rivers," the Punjab was a fertile farming province in northern India that is now divided between India and Pakistan. Although the immigrants were often called "Hindus" or "Hindoos" in America, many of them were not followers of Hinduism, one of the major religions of India. Some of them were Hindus and some were Muslims, followers

*Leaving
India*

of the Islamic faith, but most were Sikhs. Their religion was Sikhism, a blend of elements from Hinduism and Islam. Sikhs from the Punjab were highly regarded as soldiers by the British rulers of India. Many Sikhs joined army regiments led by British officers, and Sikh soldiers served throughout the British Empire.

Sikh men had several distinctive characteristics. To demonstrate their religious commitment, they never shaved their beards or cut their hair. They wore turbans, for their faith required them to cover their heads in their temples. Many of them shared the name Singh (lion), a sacred name to Sikhs. Of all the immigrants in America, said immigrant Saint N. Singh in 1909, the Sikhs had the most striking and unusual

This private in the famous Bengal Lancers was one of many Indian troops who served the British against Chinese nationalists in the Boxer Rebellion of 1900.

19

appearance. They could be seen "clad in countless curious styles." Yards upon yards of cotton or silk were wound about their heads in turbans, cone-shaped or round like button mushrooms, with waves or points directly in the middle of their foreheads or to the right or left. Singh said that the styles of turbans were as varied as the styles of American women's hairdos.

The Sikhs and other immigrants from India had many reasons for leaving their homeland. India had been a colony of Great Britain since the middle of the 18th century. The British government wanted to run India's agriculture on Western lines, with large farms and plantations instead of the small family holdings that had been the custom in India for centuries. The traditional rules of land ownership were changed by the colonial administrators, and small landholders found themselves in trouble. To pay their taxes and debts, many of them had to mortgage their land. Greedy and crooked moneylenders made the peasant farmers sign mortgage contracts that charged high interest rates. If the farmers could not make their payments, they were forced to sell their land—a disaster that happened to many hardworking families.

To make matters worse, famine devastated India from 1899 to 1902. Food was scarce. Cattle died, plunging the peasants deeper into debt. Then, in 1907, plague struck, killing half a million people in the Punjab alone. Throughout these troubled years, hundreds of thousands of Indian men left their homeland in the hope of escaping poverty and misery. They went to work in British-held territory in the West Indies, Australia, Hong Kong, Uganda (in Africa), Mauritius (an island in the Indian Ocean), and Guiana (in South Amserica).

Several thousand of them went to Canada and the United States. "Do you wonder when you look at India, with its low wages and high taxes, its famines and plagues, its absence of all incentive toward advancement, that the dam which for so long has held the people in check is weakening?" observed a writer in the *Pacific Monthly Magazine* in 1907. "Do you wonder that the East Indians are turning their faces westward toward the land of progress and opportunity?"

Some of the emigrants went to other parts of Asia before coming to America. A number of Sikh soldiers in

Famine, starvation, and poverty blighted the lives of some Indians, pushing them to seek work and better fortunes outside their homeland.

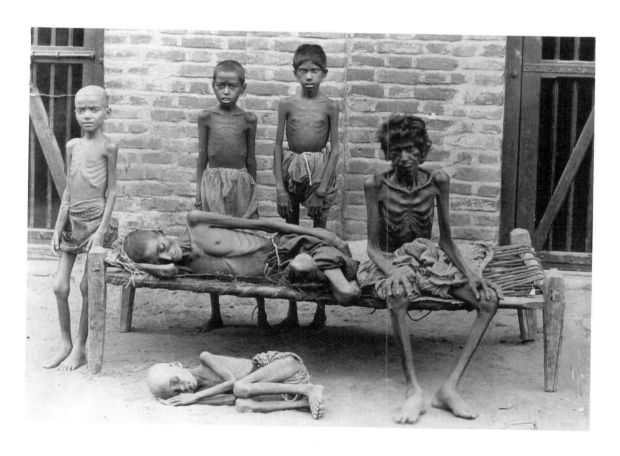

Signs identify a water fountain for Muslims and a room to rent for Hindus—followers of two of India's major faiths—reflecting deep-rooted religious conflicts in the homeland. Many early immigrants to North America belonged to a third faith, Sikhism, which was rooted in northern India.

British service were sent to China in 1900 to fight in the Boxer Rebellion, an uprising that pitted Chinese nationalists against several foreign armies, and from there some of them moved on to Canada or the United States. One Sikh soldier whose military service gave him the idea of emigrating was Puna Singh. During his three years in the army, he heard exciting stories about America. They inspired him to go to the United States in 1906, when he was 18 years old. Other Indians had been recruited to work as policemen in the British colony of Hong Kong. "I was born in the Punjabi district of India and served on the police force in Hong Kong, China, for some years," Sucha Singh told an interviewer in 1924. "While I was in China several Hindus returned and reported on the ease with which they could make money in America and so I decided to go."

These Indians regarded themselves as temporary sojourners in North America, not as permanent settlers. They had crossed the ocean to work and save money, always planning to return to India. When asked why he had left the Punjab, Deal Singh Madhas told an interviewer, "To make money and then return to the Punjab and farm for myself instead of on the ancestral property."

Most of the emigrants were the second or youngest sons, sent by their fathers to earn money to pay family debts and mortgages. Traditionally, life in India revolved around the family, which included aunts, uncles, and cousins as well as more immediate relatives. The men who emigrated from India did not go as solitary wanderers. Instead, they went abroad under the sponsorship of their families. They emigrated not so much to fulfill their own desires or hopes, but to carry out kinship duties. The decision to leave home was generally not an individual choice but rather a group decision, based on the family's needs.

To pay for their transportation to Canada or the United States, many emigrants mortgaged one or two acres of their land in India. Even if they had to go into debt to get to America, they thought the promise of getting ahead by working in the new land was worth the sacrifice. They earned only 10 or 15 cents a day in India, but they were told they would be paid as much as 2 dollars for a day's work in America.

Tuly Singh Johl used the money he had received from his brothers to pay for his passage to America. He said farewell to his family and joined the trickle of immigrants who were making their way to the port city of Calcutta. Those who came from the Punjab, like Tuly Singh Johl, traveled on foot to the nearest railway stop and then by train to Delhi, in north-central India. From Delhi they took another train to Calcutta, where they boarded vessels bound for Hong Kong. Often they had to spend a month or more in Hong Kong, waiting for a steamship to carry them to Vancouver or San Francisco. The Sikhs fared better during this waiting period than some of the other emigrants from India, for Sikhs followed the custom of building temples wherever they settled, and the Hong Kong Sikh community had established a temple. By custom, Sikh travelers could sleep there for free; they also received a free meal each day.

Along with other Sikh emigrants, Tuly Singh Johl then boarded a ship from Hong Kong bound for Vancouver, a bustling port city in the province of British Columbia on Canada's Pacific coast. Vancouver was the main point of entry for those who came to Canada from India. British Columbia was blessed with mighty forests, and its timber industry needed laborers. The morning after he arrived in Vancouver, Tuly Singh Johl was working in a lumber mill. His sojourn in America had begun.

Sikh workers at a lumber mill in British Columbia in the early 20th century.

MANY ASIAN INDIANS CHOSE CANADA AS THEIR DESTINA-
tion because both Canada and India were part of the British
Empire. In Canada, they found themselves in a world very
different from the crowded, sun-baked plains of the Punjab.
Cool and rainy British Columbia was a big, rugged province
that still had a frontier flavor in the early years of the 20th
century.

The first Asian Indians in British Columbia were a
handful of Sikh soldiers who settled on the Pacific coast in
the late 1890s. In 1902, they were joined by six Sikh policemen from Hong Kong. These early immigrants found good
jobs, earning $1.50 a day. They wrote to their families in
India, and their good reports circulated among the Punjabi
villages, sparking interest in emigration. The Canadian steamship companies helped, too. Eager for paying passengers, the
companies passed out brochures describing Canada as a land
of opportunity. The response was quick and enthusiastic. By
the end of 1903, British Columbia had received about 2,500
immigrants from India. Hundreds more arrived in the years
that followed.

Most immigrants left Vancouver as soon as they could
for jobs in the lumber camps and railroad camps that were
scattered about the western part of the province. The men
worked in sawmills or in the labor gangs that cleared land for
railroads and construction, cutting trees and brush and then
digging or blasting the huge stumps out of the ground. Those
who spoke English might get jobs as foremen of the work
gangs. All of them lived in bunkhouses and traveled from place
to place as their labor was needed. Their possessions were
limited to what they could carry with them: clothing, blankets,
perhaps a brass lamp, and a kettle.

27

Those who did not immediately get jobs lingered in Vancouver. But this fast-growing city was becoming over-crowded, and housing was scarce. The Indians also discovered that many white residents were prejudiced against Asians—not just against people from China and Japan but also against immigrants from India. Anti-Asian feeling was so strong that many whites refused to hire Indians, to rent rooms to them, or to sell goods to them in shops. By 1906, there were 500 unemployed Asian Indians in Vancouver. In dire straits, some of them sought emergency shelter in tents or abandoned buildings. An immigration official in Vancouver reported on their sad state, "It is a shame these Hindus are treated as they have been. They all have money in their pockets to pay for whatever they get, but the trouble is they can't get it." It seemed that Canadians were friendly toward the Indians in India—but not on Canadian soil. "British Columbians are proud of India . . . proud of East Indians as boys of the flag," declared a Vancouver newspaper in 1906. "But an East Indian in Canada is out of place."

White Canadian workers also complained about the entry of Asian Indians, saying, "British Columbia is a white man's country. The coming hordes of Asiatic laborers will keep wages down and crowd the white man to the wall, since a white man cannot nor will not come down to the Asiatic laborer's low standard of living." One white lumber worker expressed the fear and hostility that others up and down the Pacific coast felt toward the Asian Indians when he blustered, "One of these days, by God, the whites are going to chase all of them out of camp and they won't come back either. We'll drive them all down the line with a two-by-four."

The number of Chinese and Japanese immigrants who could enter Canada had already been strictly limited by law. Now the exclusionists—people who wanted to exclude Asians, or keep them out of the country—started calling for laws to keep out immigrants from India as well. Vancouver's exclusionists sang in the streets:

> *For white man's land we fight.*
> *To Oriental grasp and greed*
> *We'll surrender, no, never.*
> *Our watchword be "God save the King,"*
> *White Canada for ever.*

Angry exclusionists marched to the docks in October 1906 when a ship called *Empress of Japan* came into port. Aboard the ship were a number of Asian Indians who planned to enter Canada. Vancouver's mayor, who supported the exclusionists, ordered the police to surround the immigration buildings, imprisoning the immigrants. The mayor sent a telegram to the premier of Canada, saying, "City of Vancouver will not stand for any further dumping of East Indians here." At an emotional town meeting, a retired army officer who spoke up to defend the immigrants' rights was shouted down by cries of "Canada is a white man's country!" A city official suggested that the best way to deal with the immigrants was to let them die of hunger and cold. Finally, after three days, the immigrants were released, but the federal government of Canada realized that something had to be done to ease the tension in British Columbia.

Canada's central government did not agree with the exclusionists that Asian immigrants should be kept from entering the country. Federal officials realized that, as part of the British Empire, Canada was expected to honor the rights of all subjects of the empire, including Indians. Throughout India, people were objecting ever more strongly to the way they were discriminated against by the British, both in their own country and throughout the empire. The Indian nationalist movement had begun to call for independence from British rule. Leaders in Great Britain and Canada knew that anti-Indian discrimination in Canada added fuel to the fire of nationalism in India. As one newspaper put it: "A blow struck at a Hindu in Canada may be felt by a white man in India." But these imperial concerns did not mean much to the agitated citizens of British Columbia, where most of Canada's Asian Indian immigrants were located. A combination of racial prejudice and fear of losing their jobs to foreign workers had turned many British Columbians into exclusionists.

The tension flared into violence in September 1907, when several ships carrying Chinese, Japanese, and Sikh immigrants landed in Vancouver. A crowd of about 10,000 exclusionists marched on city hall, bearing signs that read "Stand for a white Canada." The protest turned into a riot when the marchers surged through Vancouver's Chinatown, throwing rocks and starting fires. No lives were lost, but there was considerable property damage. The next day, a crowd blocked the streets when port officials tried to escort 900 Indian immigrants off their ship. Police could not clear the crowd, and the Indians were forced to return to their ship. Eventually the immigrants were allowed to land, but the riot had made it clear that British Columbia did not welcome Asian Indians. The governments of Canada and Great Britain began working to discourage Indians from going to Canada.

Canada passed a series of immigration laws that severely limited the ability of Indians to enter the country; new rules also gave officials in British Columbia the right to turn away any immigrants they did not want to admit. More than 2,600 Asian Indians had come to Canada in 1907–8, but in the three years that followed, only 21 entered. The stream of migration from India had become a tiny trickle.

The exclusionists had won the fight to keep new Asian Indian immigrants out of Canada, but they were not satisfied with this victory. They also wanted to get rid of the Indians who were already in Canada. Several plans were proposed. The Sikhs were encouraged to emigrate to Hawaii or Honduras, but these attempts failed. The small Asian Indian community in Canada remained settled, even though, as one Sikh sadly explained, the immigrants had come to see that "the white man has two standards, one for his own use and the other for the man with the brown skin."

Historian Joan M. Jensen, who chronicled the experience of these early immigrants in her 1988 book *Passage from India: Asian Indian Immigrants in North America*, explains that the Canadian Sikhs "might have become a small, forgotten colony" if not for "their determination to obtain equal rights

The Komagata Maru *in Vancouver harbor. Sikhs aboard the ship challenged Canada's exclusion laws but eventually returned to India in defeat.*

31

with other Canadian immigrants." The fight for equal rights centered around the families that the immigrants had left behind in India. After working hard and saving their money for several years, some of the men could afford to send for their wives and children—but the exclusion laws would not let the families enter the country. The Sikhs complained to the central government in Ottawa, without results. In 1914, the exclusion laws were renewed.

A letter written in 1914 on behalf of 600 Sikhs in Hong Kong, addressed to their friends in America, expressed their fear of the laws that would keep them out of Canada. The letter said, "For God's sake, help us get to the United States or Canada. The new Canadian law will go into effect on 5 March 1914 after which time few Hindus will be admitted into Canada. It has been much more difficult for the past six months to get into Manila than heretofore. We are shut out of Australia and New Zealand. For God's sake, come to our assistance so that we will be able to get into the United States or Canada."

Canada's immigration laws were challenged later in 1914, when a wealthy Sikh named Gurdit Singh hired a ship called the *Komagata Maru* to carry 376 immigrants from India to Vancouver. Singh told Canadian reporters, "We are British citizens and we consider we have a right to visit any part of the Empire. We are determined to make this a test case and if we are refused entrance into your country, the matter will not end there. Other boats will be chartered and my people will continue to cross the Pacific until we secure what we consider to be our rights." But officials in Vancouver would not allow the *Komagata Maru* to dock.

The ship remained in the harbor for three months while the Indians tried to win the right to come ashore and white exclusionists on shore insisted that they be kept out. Finally, after several skirmishes between harbor police and the would-be immigrants, the Canadian navy ordered the *Komagata Maru* to leave Canadian waters. Gurdit Singh and his comrades returned to India. The treatment they had received in Canada was "resented all over India," said Jawaharlal Nehru, later to become the first prime minister of independent India. The incident left Sikhs in both India and North America more bitter than ever against white rule.

For the next few decades, Canada kept strict limits on immigration from India. Many of the earlier immigrants left Canada, either returning to India or moving south to the United States in search of better prospects. By 1932, the Asian Indian population of British Columbia had dwindled to only 720. Then matters began to improve slowly. In 1938, Asians living in British Columbia won the right to vote in elections there. In 1952, a new federal immigration law allowed 250 Asian Indians to enter Canada each year. Some wives and children were able to come from India to join the men from whom they had been separated for many years.

Gradually, a community of families began to form. Then, in 1967, Canada's immigration law was revised again. At long last, Asian Indians were permitted to immigrate in numbers equal to those of other countries. Since that time, despite some incidents of racial discrimination, Canada has officially held to its vision of society as a "cultural mosaic," in which a group can retain its ethnicity and still be part of a larger national identity.

*Because of the distinctive Sikh headgear, the flow of immigrants from India
to the western United States was called "the tide of turbans."*

VERY FEW ASIAN INDIANS CAME TO THE UNITED STATES before 1906. A handful of Asian Indians made their way to New England in the late 18th century on Massachusetts sailing ships that had docked in India, and during the 19th century a few prospectors and merchants from India appeared in California. In addition, Indian religious leaders visited Boston and other East Coast cities, where they found cultured audiences eager to listen to their talks on the ancient faiths of Hinduism and Buddhism. Large-scale immigration began in 1906, when 600 Asian Indians applied to enter the United States; many of them came from Vancouver, rather than directly from India.

This period of Asian Indian immigration into the United States was extremely short. In 1909, U.S. immigration officials began limiting immigration from India, and eight years later Congress banned it completely. Altogether, only 6,400 people came to the United States during this first wave of immigration from India.

Unlike the Chinese and Japanese immigrants who had come before them, the Asian Indians did not develop an ethnic community with geographical boundaries. The Chinese had their Chinatowns in American cities, and the Japanese their Little Tokyos, but the Asian Indians did not form an India-town. They were a small population, mostly spread out in little groups up and down the West Coast. Their story is an especially interesting and important part of the history of Asian Americans, for they were a new kind of immigrant. Like their Asian brethren, they were "strangers from a different shore," from Asia rather than from Europe. But unlike the Japanese and Chinese, the Asian Indians were classified as belonging to the Caucasian or white race.

35

One Asian Indian immigrant described his fellow newcomers this way:

> All Hindoos who come to America have hair varying in hue from brownish-black to purplish or an intense raven-black. . . . The hide of the Hindoo varies from the dull, pale, sallow-brown of a Mexican to the extreme black of an African. . . . They have intelligent faces, keen eyes, compressed lips and determined chins. This type of countenance is distinctly Aryan, as all Hindoos who come to the land of the Stars and Stripes are descended from the same branch of the human family as the Anglo-Saxons.

As with the immigrants to Canada, the majority of the Asian Indians who came to the United States were Sikhs. They were easily recognized by their uncut hair and beards and by the turbans that most of them continued to wear, although some adopted Western-style suits or shirts and trousers. Their traditional headgear caused the Sikh immigrants to be described as "a tide of turbans." One observer wrote, "Always the turban remains, the badge and symbol of their native land, their native customs and religion. Whether repairing tracks on the long stretches of the Northern Pacific railways, feeding logs into the screaming rotary saws of the lumber-mills, picking fruit in the luxuriant orchards or sunny hillsides of California, the twisted turban shows white or brilliant . . . an exotic thing in the western landscape."

Their turbans and their dark skin brought the Sikhs taunts and verbal abuse from whites. They were called by insulting names such as "rag-heads" and treated as inferior beings. One California Sikh recounted, "I used to go to

Marysville every Saturday. One day a drunk *ghora* (white man) came out of a bar and motioned to me saying, 'Come here, slave!' I said I was no slave man. He told me that his race ruled India and America, too."

Whites sometimes associated the Asian Indian immigrants with blacks, Chinese, or Japanese. Often the Asian Indians were lumped together with other Asian peoples as "Asiatics," whom prejudiced whites considered unfit to be part of American society. Samuel L. Gompers, a leader of the American labor movement, said in 1908, "Sixty years' contact with the Chinese, and twenty-five years' experience with the Japanese and two or three years' acquaintance with Hindus should be sufficient to convince any ordinarily intelligent person that they have no standards...." The Asians were often blamed for the violence directed against them by whites, who knew nothing of Asian peoples and often misinterpreted their behavior. "In California the insolence and presumption of Japanese, and the immodest and filthy habits of the Hindoos are continually involving them in trouble, beatings.... In all these cases, we may say the Oriental is at fault," declared the Asiatic Exclusion League, an organization whose goal was to keep Asian immigrants out of the western states.

In a 1908 magazine article called "The West and the Hindu Invasion," a writer named Agnes Foster Buchanan described three waves of Asian immigrants that had "threatened" American society. First came the Chinese, but an 1882 exclusion law had ended Chinese immigration. Then came immigrants from Japan, and while white Americans were wondering what should be done about the Japanese, they suddenly noticed another group of "strangers"—the "Hindus." "Tall of stature, straight of feature, swarthy of color,"

*These Indian men adopted
North American clothing
and hairstyles but continued
to smoke the traditional
Indian water pipe. Asian
and American ways were
blended in the lives of
many immigrants.*

the Asian Indians were unlike the Chinese and Japanese in an important way, Buchanan admitted: They were "brothers" of the white race. But like the Chinese and Japanese, the Asian Indians were eager to work and willing to accept lower wages than many whites; this made them a threat to white workers, who felt that the competition was unfair. Buchanan called for laws to exclude Asian Indians from the United States, urging white Americans "to tell our brothers of the East" that while the earth is large enough for everyone, Caucasians of European and Indian descent could not live comfortably together in any one part of it.

Asian Indians were especially feared as labor competitors by white workers. Many of them were victimized by white working-class hostility and violence. One of the worst incidents took place in September 1907, when several hundred white workers in Bellingham, Washington, armed themselves with clubs, took the law into their own hands, and drove 700 Asian Indians across the border into Canada. Two months later, white workers forcibly rounded up Asian Indians in Everett, Washington, and expelled them from the town. In both towns, police turned their backs as Indians were beaten and their belongings were stolen by the mobs.

In San Francisco, the Asiatic Exclusion League warned of the new "menace" from India. The league said that the Asian Indian immigrants were competitors for white men's jobs and were also dirty, lustful, and diseased. "From every part of the Coast," the league claimed, "complaints are made of the undesirability of the Hindoos, their lack of cleanliness, disregard of sanitary laws, petty pilfering, especially of chickens, and insolence to women."

U.S. immigration officials responded to the growing pressure from the anti-Asian exclusionists. Between 1908 and 1920, the immigration authorities turned away more than 3,400 Asian Indians who sought entry to the United States. In 1917, Congress passed a restrictive immigration law that prevented Asian Indian laborers from entering the country. Twelve years later, the Indian poet Rabindranath Tagore, a winner of the Nobel Prize in literature, traveled to North America. After lecturing in British Columbia, he decided to visit the United States. When he applied for entry to the United States, Tagore encountered difficulties, and when he finally made it into the country, he experienced racial prejudice in Los Angeles. Tagore canceled his tour and promptly returned to India, saying in disgust, "Jesus could not get into America because, first of all, He would not have the necessary money, and secondly, He would be an Asiatic."

The Asian Indians posed a special problem for America's exclusionists. The cultures of India were as alien to most white Americans as the cultures of China and Japan. But the deeper difficulty was racial. Whereas some Asian Indians were light-skinned, others were dark in complexion. Nevertheless, unlike the Chinese and Japanese, Asian Indians were considered to be Caucasian. This raised the question of whether Asian Indians could become citizens of the United States.

A federal law dating from 1790 said that only "white persons" could become naturalized citizens. (The process by which immigrants become citizens of their new country is called naturalization, and immigrants who receive citizenship are called naturalized citizens.) This 1790 law had prevented

Known as "Hindu Halls," these workers' houses at the Hammond Sawmill on the Columbia River near Astoria, Oregon, were occupied mainly by Asian Indians working at the mill in the 1920s.

Chinese, Japanese, Korean, and Filipino immigrants from claiming U.S. citizenship.

The law was challenged by a Japanese immigrant named Takao Ozawa, who was determined to prove his right to citizenship. Ozawa filed an application for United States citizenship in 1914, but his request was rejected. He challenged the rejection in federal court in Hawaii, and the court ruled that Ozawa could not become a citizen. The court declared that Ozawa was "in every way eminently qualified under the statutes to become an American citizen"—except in one way. He was not white.

Again Ozawa challenged the ruling, taking his case all the way to the U.S. Supreme Court in 1922. Ozawa told the court that he was a person of good character, honest and industrious. He did not drink liquor, smoke, or gamble. More important, "at heart" he was "a true American." His family belonged to an American church. His children went to an American school. Loyal to the United States, Ozawa said he was grateful to "our Uncle Sam" for the opportunity the country had given him. But Ozawa lost his case. He was not entitled to become a citizen, said the Supreme Court, because he was "not Caucasian." He was barred from citizenship by the 1790 law that limited citizenship to members of the white race.

Asian Indians believed that they should not be denied citizenship by that law. In their opinion, they were Caucasians, and they were white. Therefore, they reasoned, they should be allowed to become naturalized citizens. Indeed, some Asian Indian immigrants had already managed to become naturalized citizens. Others who had applied for citizenship, however, had been turned down.

41

The tangled question of race and citizenship for Asian Indians went to the U.S. Supreme Court in 1923, the year after the *Ozawa* case. An immigrant from India named Bhagat Singh Thind argued that as a member of the Caucasian race he was eligible for citizenship. But the court destroyed the hopes of Thind and his fellow immigrants by ruling that the term "white person" meant an immigrant from Europe. Although Asian Indians and Europeans might have been racially related "in the dim reaches of antiquity," said the court, they were now separate. In the view of the "common man," Asian Indians were not "white persons." Their bid for citizenship was turned down. In addition, they were turned away from government aid programs during the severe economic depression of the 1930s because they were aliens who were not eligible for citizenship.

With their hopes dashed by the *Thind* case and the Great Depression, some Asian Indian immigrants returned to India. Soon after the Supreme Court had turned down Thind's bid for citizenship, an Asian Indian immigrant wrote his friend Puna Singh in India, advising Singh to stay in India. Singh had come to the United States once before, in 1906. He had become a naturalized citizen in 1920, before the *Thind* decision made it impossible for Asian Indians to apply for citizenship. Singh then returned to India, where he married a woman named Nand Kaur. Years later, Puna Singh's daughter recalled how the *Thind* decision had affected her father. "My father's friend sent him a letter to tell him about the *Thind* decision and warn him not to try to return to America with his wife," Jane Singh said. "The decision meant my father was no longer a citizen and could not reenter this country. But the letter did not arrive in time." As it turned out, Puna Singh managed to return to the United States with his bride, but shortly afterward, the United States canceled the citizenship that had already been granted to Singh and a number of other Asian Indians. Singh was angry that he had been forced to become "a citizen of no country."

The life of immigrant Vaisho Das Bagai was tragically altered by the loss of his citizenship. He had arrived in the United States with his family in 1915 and had become a naturalized citizen. After his citizenship was taken away, Bagai took his life. In his suicide note, he wrote that he had tried to be "as American as possible." He went on: "But now they come to me and say, I am no longer an American citizen. . . . What have I made of myself and my children? We cannot exercise our rights, we cannot leave this country. Humility and insults, who are responsible for all this? I do not choose to live a life of an interned person. . . . Is life worth living in a gilded cage? Obstacles this way, blockades that way, and the bridges burnt behind."

A year after the *Thind* decision, Congress passed the 1924 Immigration Act. This law banned all immigration by people who could not become naturalized citizens—a restriction that was designed to keep out immigrants from China, Japan, Korea, and also India. The flow of newcomers from India was cut off.

The *Thind* decision also affected the lives of Asian Indians who had already settled in the United States—not only by allowing their citizenship to be taken away, but in other ways as well. Some states such as California had laws against racial intermarriage. These laws prevented Asian Indian men, who were considered nonwhite, from marrying white women.

Property rights were also affected by the *Thind* decision. Asian Indian immigrants could no longer own land in states where land ownership was limited to people with the right to become naturalized citizens. In California, for example, the Alien Land Law stated that no immigrant who was ineligible to become a U.S. citizen could buy or lease land. Soon after the Supreme Court decided the *Thind* case, the attorney general of California took action to cancel Asian Indian land purchases. A Sacramento newspaper applauded the ruling against Asian Indians, saying, "There must be no more leasing or sale of land to such immigrants from India."

An Asian Indian in California sadly noted that his people—as well as other Asian immigrants such as the Japanese—could no longer farm their own land or operate businesses. They "either must take to day labor or get out of the country." Some had already left the United States. Even before the *Thind* decision, Asian Indians had begun a return migration to India.

One of the early immigrants, Haji Muhammad Sharif Khan, left the United States for India in 1920. He had heard about opportunities in America while serving in the British police force in Hong Kong, and he had arrived in San Francisco, full of hope, in 1903. First he worked on a railroad near Sacramento; then he became a farm laborer. In 1914, he leased land to raise chickens; within a few years, he had 14,000 chickens. Khan's poultry business made high profits during World War I (1914–18), when the demand for food was high. After the war, Khan bought a one-way ticket to India, returning to his homeland with the money he had earned and

saved in California. About half of all the Asian Indian immi-grants followed his example. Between 1920 and 1940, 3,000 of them returned to India.

Meanwhile, the anti-British independence movement was gaining strength in India. The independence movement found support in Asian Indian communities in the United States, where many immigrants were bitter about the barriers that whites had placed to prevent Asian Indians from immi-grating freely and becoming citizens. Students played an important role in the nationalist or independence movement. In 1908, Taraknath Das, a student at the University of Washington, began publishing a nationalist newspaper called *Free Hindustan.* Three years later, Asian Indian intellectuals in San Francisco organized the Ghadr party (*ghadr* means "revo-lution" or "mutiny" in Urdu, the main language of north India). They spread their revolutionary message through a weekly newspaper called *Ghadr;* they also visited Asian Indians in Sacramento, Fresno, and Stockton, urging their country-

Members of the Sikh community in California around 1910. Newcomers from India were concentrated in the West Coast states of California, Oregon, and Washington.

men to support the nationalist cause. A U.S. immigration official reported in 1914, "Most of the Indian students are infected with seditious ideas. Even Sikhs of the laboring class have not escaped their influence."

The Ghadr movement inspired nationalism among Asian Indians in America. They sang songs protesting Britain's domination of their "mother country":

> *Alas, dear country, to what*
> *condition hast thou been reduced!*
> *Your whole shape has become deformed, your*
> *downfall is near.*
> *Your whole house has been destroyed and the*
> *Goddess of Wealth looted.*
> *Dear Mother, you are continuously robbed by*
> *the British.*

The message of Ghadr was especially meaningful to Asian Indians in the United States. They saw a link between the way they were discriminated against in America and the fact that their homeland had been taken over by the British. Another protest song lamented the loss of national dignity and pride:

> *Some push us around, some curse us.*
> *Where is your splendor and prestige today?*
> *The whole world calls us black thieves,*
> *The whole world calls us "coolie."*
> *Why doesn't our flag fly anywhere?*
> *Why do we feel low and humiliated?*
> *Why is there no respect for us in the whole world?*

The nationalists felt that independence for India would not only bring justice in the homeland but would bring repect for Asian Indians in America. Many Asian Indians in the United States were deeply committed to the struggle for Indian independence. In the fall of 1914, after the outbreak of World War I, 400 Asian Indians left America to join a Ghadr uprising in India. But the uprising failed, and the Ghadr movement quickly collapsed. The Ghadr party in the United States was destroyed in 1917 when the U.S. government, under pressure from Great Britain, jailed several Asian Indians on charges of conspiracy.

Workers from India helped build railroads through the rugged mountains of northern California. Railroad work provided a livelihood for many Asian Indian immigrants until violence from white workers drove them away from their jobs.

Chapter Four

Working in America

ALTHOUGH ASIAN INDIAN IMMIGRANTS IN THE UNITED States were interested in the political events that were taking place in India, most of them were mainly concerned about their condition in America. They had come to the United States with high hopes, expecting to make their fortunes, but they discovered that life in America was unexpectedly challenging. Many of them encountered prejudice, born of ignorance and fear. Some found it hard to get work. And those who had jobs lived a life very different from the life they had known in India. Instead of belonging to a settled community of families, they traveled from place to place with their work gangs. And although most of them had been farmers or farm laborers in the Punjab, in America they often had to turn to other kinds of work.

Tuly Singh Johl, the immigrant from Jundialla who had arrived in Vancouver in 1907, was one of many Asian Indians who came south to the United States from Canada. Upon arriving in Canada, he had found a job in a lumber camp in British Columbia, but soon he and three other Sikh laborers left for Bellingham, Washington, to join friends from India who were working there. Johl worked in a sawmill outside Bellingham for seven months—until anti-Asian feelings stirred up by the exclusionists broke out in the riot against Asian Indians in Bellingham. Johl's boss was afraid that his mill would be burned by angry white workers, so he fired Johl and 20 other Sikhs.

Johl and the others went south by train to California; they had heard that there were jobs building railroads there. Many Asian Indian immigrants in California and Washington had found work on the railways. In Tacoma, Washington, Asian Indians were used as replacements for Italian rail workers who had gone on strike. "For miles their turbaned figures may be seen wielding crow-bar or shovel along the tracks," a magazine reported in 1910.

In northern California, as many as 2,000 Asian Indians worked beside Italian, Chinese, Japanese, Scandinavian, and Korean laborers to build the Western Pacific Railroad across the Sierra Nevada mountain range. About 700 Sikhs worked on the longest tunnel on the line, the three-mile-long Spring Garden Tunnel along the Feather River. Tuly Singh Johl worked for the Western Pacific, first leveling land for the train station in Marysville and later laying track up in the hills. He worked with other Sikhs, but Greek and Chinese gangs worked nearby; Johl later remembered that the various ethnic groups had been friendly toward one another.

Within a few years, however, Asian Indians were driven out of the railroad and lumber industries by violent white workers. The Sikhs moved south, riding the Southern Pacific Railroad into central California, where they found employment in agriculture. Many California farmers were eager to hire Asian Indians because immigration laws had cut off the supply of Chinese and Japanese labor. Farmers turned to Asian Indians to reduce the labor shortage. Along with many of his fellow immigrants, Tuly Singh Johl turned to agriculture when his railroad job ended. He and four friends from Jundialla went to Fresno to pick grapes in the vineyards.

In northern California, 500 Punjabis worked in the Newcastle fruit district east of Sacramento in 1908, and 300 more picked fruit in the nearby Vaca Valley. Asian Indian farm laborers quickly spread throughout the Sacramento Valley, working on fruit farms and rice farms. They moved into the San Joaquin Valley, where they worked in the grape and celery fields and cleared land for new fields. Some 600 of them were employed on citrus farms. From the San Joaquin Valley, Asian Indians entered the Imperial Valley, gathering cantaloupes and picking cotton. A grower told an interviewer in 1930, "We are using Hindus for cleaning our ditches." He went on to explain that Chinese laborers had gotten too old for such strenuous work, and Japanese laborers did not want to do it. "You can't get the younger generations of these peoples into any of this common work," the grower said. "But the Hindus are very efficient at this work."

Asian Indian farm laborers were organized into gangs, with anywhere from 3 to 50 laborers in each gang. The gang leader, who was usually the one who spoke English the best, received a payment from the other members for arranging their work and was also paid a wage by the employer. The leader was responsible for finding jobs, bargaining with the employer to set the terms of labor, arranging for the workers' food and lodging, and serving as general supervisor.

The labor gangs became substitute families for the Asian Indians, far from their home communities in a strange and sometimes hostile land. Often the gangs included men who were related to one another or who came from the same village or region. Members shared the same religion, language, background, and goals. Without wives and families, the men came to depend on the gangs for companionship and security. As members of a gang, they worked together, traveled together, lived and ate together, and shared expenses and sorrows. They felt close bonds to one another. When a member died, the rest joined together to pay for the funeral, to send photographs of the body back to India, and to give money to the dead man's widow.

Punjabi farm laborers not only picked different crops depending upon the season, but they also performed a variety of other tasks. In December and January, they pruned fruit trees and grape vines. From March through May, they worked on irrigation canals and ditches. From July through October, they picked fruit. The "turbaned" workers "were continually on the wing," wrote a reporter in 1922, "coming from the melon and cotton fields in the Imperial Valley, en route to the fig orchards and vineyards of Fresno, or the rice fields near Sacramento." The Asian Indian farm workers moved around a great deal during the year. "During the grape picking season great numbers of them are in Fresno County," a California lawyer said. "At the time of rice harvesting there will be about a thousand of them near Willows; during the cotton season in Imperial Valley (this being when the weather is very hot), they go to that place for work."

Traveling in gangs from farm to farm, Punjabi laborers worked from ten to fourteen hours a day, depending on the season and the type of crop. "We got up at half past three," one of them said, describing their work in the asparagus fields, "and before the first faint daylight was visible we were ready for work." Instead of hourly wages, they received 10 cents for every full box of asparagus. Cutting asparagus was boring and tiring. "As soon as I had knelt down with my knife and cut out one head and put it in the box, there would be another one spouting before me," the worker recalled. "Then I would have to stoop again, and it was this continuous picking and stooping that made it a terrible form of exercise." All day long

it was "walk and bend, bend and walk," from half past four in the morning until seven in the evening. Every now and then the boss—"an American foreman"—would come into the asparagus fields and yell, "Hurry up! Hurry up!"

But the workers found ways to set their own pace. "We had an extraordinary boss," an Asian Indian said, "an Italian constantly swearing and spitting." This foreman thought that he could discipline his workers by shouting at them, but they played "a very clever trick" on him, tiring him out so that he would leave them alone. Explained the worker, "Whenever he shouted we worked hard and as he stopped shouting we relaxed our speed." After shouting continuously for a half hour or so, the boss would leave the fields. Then

The growing agricultural industry of the American West needed labor, and men from India filled that need after immigration laws had cut off the supply of workers from China and Japan.

*Far from their homes
and families, the Asian
Indian farm workers
lived a lonely, roving life,
traveling from place to place.*

the workers would slow down, keeping an eye open for his return. "We nearly always heard him before we saw him," the laborer recalled, "for he was noisily drunk half the day and the other half he fretted because he was not drunk."

Sometimes, too, workers would "disappear" into the trees to rest while picking fruit. Again, recalled one Punjabi, they kept alert for the foreman's return: "From our tree tops

we would see the boss coming 'way off in the distance and when he reached us he found us working very hard."

Occasionally the Asian Indians worked in the fields together with Japanese farm laborers. Tensions developed as the employers pitted the two groups against each other, hoping to make both groups work harder. Members of the different ethnic groups sometimes taunted one another. But gradually, as they labored side by side, many Japanese and Asian Indians also came to see that they were united in the brotherhood of work. They joined together to fool the foremen and growers.

Employers often paid Asian Indian workers less than they paid workers of other nationalities. The Asian Indians, however, figured out ways to get more money for their work by tinkering with the account books. For example, a gang leader might list 60 workers' names in his book and receive pay from the employer for 60 men, although only 50 had really worked on the job. Or an Asian Indian bookkeeper and gang leader would conspire to alter the figures in the books. "This form of cheating we later on called 'bonus' and we gave the name of 'bonus monger' to our bookkeeper," said one man.

The Asian Indian migrant workers' lives were sometimes harshly uncomfortable. Camping near the fields, they often slept under the stars or in tents. They were also housed in bunkhouses, barns, and sheds. Their quarters were often crowded; 12 men could be found in a single room, sleeping on the floor with blankets.

The workers generally prepared their own food, and their diet depended upon their religion. Those who were

Muslims did not eat pork. As a rule, they would not buy meat that had been prepared by other hands, so the meat they ate was usually limited to poultry and lamb that they butchered themselves. The Hindus were vegetarians and usually had their own cooks in the camps. The Sikhs ate mostly vegetables, fruit, milk, and *roti* (tortillalike cakes of bread). They consumed a lot of milk, sometimes one or two quarts a day per person. In one of the camps, an Asian Indian told a woman visitor, "We eat no meat, that is, no beef—the cow is sacred." The woman snapped, "But you drink milk? And your cow gives you the milk!" To which the man replied, "Yes, we drink our mother's milk also, but we do not eat her!" Those who came from the Punjab—where neither vegetable oil nor lard was commonly used—were used to consuming large quantities of butter, which they called *ghi*. American shopkeepers and employers were startled to see that the Punjabis used at least 15 pounds per person each month. "It's the butter that makes the food," the Punjabis said. The daughter of a Korean farmer in California remembered how much the Sikh laborers enjoyed their butter. She recalled, "They would sit around a large pot of melted butter and garlic, dipping tortillas made with flour and water into it." The Asian Indians liked their foods heavily spiced with curry, coriander, cumin, cayenne, and black pepper.

By about 1920, Asian Indian farm workers were earning wages equal to those of Japanese and white workers. By that time, a few Asian Indians had become tenant farmers, working on land owned by others but living in one place rather than moving about. Some Asian Indians had even managed to buy or lease land; they then hired others to work for them. A

California state official reported that "the Hindus are rapidly leaving the employed list and are becoming employers."

Agriculture seemed like a natural choice for the Punjabi immigrants, most of whom had been farmers in India and who came from a province known for agriculture. But not all of the Indians actually chose agriculture because of their love of farming—many were pushed into agriculture when opportunities in other kinds of work were closed to them. Farmer Dalip Singh Saund of California's Imperial Valley explained that because of racial discrimination, "few opportunities existed for me or people of my nationality in the state at the time. I was not a citizen and could not become one. The only way Indians in California could make a living . . . was to join with others who had settled in various parts of the state as farmers."

Most of the Asian Indian farmers probably started out as gang bosses. Their ability to speak English, along with their higher earnings as bosses, gave them the resources they needed to run their own farms. Partnership farming was very popular among the Punjabis. Two to eight men would put up equal amounts of money to invest in a farm, becoming equal shareholders, and one partner would manage the business. Harnam Singh Sidhu, for example, formed a partnership with several other Sikhs to lease a thousand acres for rice farming. Their expenses were high, for they had to buy a thresher, a tractor, and other rice-harvesting machinery. But their first year's crop was very successful, enabling them to pay off their debts.

The Punjabis were "excellent farmers, very industrious, willing to work under trying conditions," stated a white landlord. "In the heat of summer they got up at 4 o'clock, worked with their teams until about 10 A.M., then with the hoe until say 4 P.M. and then with their teams until 9 o'clock in the evening." By 1919, Asian Indians were renting 86,000 acres and owned 2,100 acres in California; almost all of these farms were in the Sacramento Valley and the Imperial Valley. Many of the Punjabi farmers grew crops with which they had grown familiar in India, especially cotton and rice. In the Sacramento Valley, they devoted most of their acres to rice production. Other Asian Indian farmers raised nuts, fruits, and potatoes; Jawala and Bisaka Singh, for example, became known as the "Potato Kings" of Holtville.

After the Alien Land Law of 1920 and the Supreme Court's *Thind* decision of 1923, Asian Indians were denied the right to own land in California. Some farmers who had become independent and self-employed lost their land and were forced to become laborers again. "Since the Alien Land Laws were put into effect," said a former landowner named Sucha Singh, "I have been working for others near Holtville."

But some Asian Indians were able to hold on to their land. Those who had children who had been born in the United States could register the land in their children's names, for these children were U.S. citizens and were allowed to own land. Sometimes those who did not have any American-born children could "rent" the services of other immigrants' children, such as the American-born sons of a Punjabi family who held land for various Asian Indians for a fee of one dollar per acre. But there were few American-born children among the Asian Indian immigrants.

Most of the Asian Indians who managed to own land did so through an Anglo "front man." They bought or leased land in the names of Anglo farmers, bankers, or lawyers whom they trusted. For example, when a Sikh named Munshi Singh Thiara bought 20 acres, he had an Anglo silent partner who was the legal owner of the property. In 1925, Imam Bakhash, his son Kalu Khan, and his partner Atta Muhammad leased 2,000 acres, but their Anglo attorney actually leased the land for them in his own name and in return received a share of their crop. Babu Khan and his brother Naimat Khan leased 2,000 acres in 1928 by using their lawyer as the front man. Harnam Singh Sidhu bought 45 acres of land under the name of an Anglo friend and called the arrangement a "dummy partnership." Said one Sikh, "Many of our American friends bought land for us under their names, and so we were able to carry on farming." The director of the Holtville National Bank held land for so many Punjabi clients that his bank became known as the "Hindu Bank." Punjabis also formed corporations with Anglos, an arrangement that let them skirt the law and farm their own land.

The desire to own land in the United States showed that a change had taken place in the attitudes of the Asian Indian immigrants. In the early years, Asian Indians had come to the United States to work temporarily and then return to their homeland. But something happened—they became settlers instead of sojourners. They saw themselves spending the rest of their lives in America. As early as 1910, according to an immigration report, only about half of the Asian Indians who entered the country said that they were planning to return to India. The others were uncertain about their plans—or, in a number of cases, they had decided to stay in the United States. Despite the difficulties they encountered, they felt that

As the Asian Indian immigrants became settlers in America, a community took root. Asian Indians built temples, and restaurants and other businesses, such as this store in Honolulu.

life in America had more to offer than they could expect in their homeland.

One Asian Indian immigrant summed up the feelings of many when he told an interviewer in 1922 that he had left the Punjab "so long ago," meaning 10 or 12 years:

"Are you homesick?" the interviewer asked.

"Not any longer," the man replied. "One adjusts oneself."

"Are you going back to the Punjab?"

The immigrant shrugged, smiled, and then replied, "I make more money here."

A traditional Indian wedding ceremony. Such events were rare among the early immigrants in America. Many of the men had wives and children in India; those who were single had almost no chance of meeting an Asian Indian woman to marry.

Chapter Five

A Community of "Uncles"

EVEN AFTER THE IMMIGRANTS HAD DECIDED TO RE-main in the United States as settlers, there were very few Asian Indian families in America. Almost all of the immigrants were men. In 31914, only one-quarter of 1% of the Asian Indians in California were women. An unmarried Asian Indian man in America had no chance of meeting an unmarried Asian Indian woman and starting a family.

At first, the men had planned to be in the United States only temporarily, and they had given little thought to the shortage of women. Many of them, in fact, already had wives in India. Of the married immigrants who had left their wives in their homeland, many had mortgaged their farms in India to pay for their passage to America. They had been too deeply in debt to consider bringing their wives and children with them.

One-third to one-half of the immigrants had left families behind in India. In 1909, a survey of 474 Asian Indians by immigration officials showed that 31 were wid-owed, 228 were single, and 215 were married to women in India. That same year, immigrant Saint N. Singh wrote:

> One of the chief points of difference between the emigrant from India and those hailing from Europe lies in the fact that the European brings along with him his family—his wife and children . . . —when he emigrates to America. Only one sex is represented among the Hindoo immigrants. Probably the greater percentage of them are married—for Hindoos marry young—but they leave their wives and children be-hind them and venture alone to find a fortune in the West. There is only one Hindoo woman on the North

American continent. She lives with her husband, a doctor of Vedic medicine, in Vancouver, B.C.

As Asian Indians established themselves in the United States, they yearned for family life. The married men wanted to send for their families; the unmarried ones hoped to bring women from India to marry. A handful of wives did arrive. One of them was Nand Kaur Singh, who later recalled her first home in an isolated apple orchard in Utah: "When we got there it was II at night. We went for a walk. . . . And then I started crying. I said, 'What's wrong with India?' And he said, 'You will like it here soon.'" But, she added, the adjustment was not easy. In America, she felt a loneliness that she had never known in India. "I had come from a village where I was surrounded by family and friends, and here there was no one but my husband, who worked hard all day. . . . There were none of my countrywomen to speak with, and it was against our custom to talk with men who were not related."

Altogether, only a very few Asian Indian women came to America. Even this tiny flow stopped in 1917, when a new immigration law placed restrictions on Asian Indian immigration. After that time, men with wives in India could no longer bring them into the United States. Many Punjabi men dreamed of returning to India for their wives and bringing them back to the United States, but they were afraid to try. Said Bagga Singh Sunga, "I knew that if I went back to India to join her, we would never be allowed to come back to the United States."

With no Asian Indian women available, some of the unmarried immigrants chose to marry outside their ethnic group. Punjabi men who wished to marry white women faced legal and social barriers. In many places, marriage between people of different races was prohibited by law. County clerks in California, deciding that these laws applied to Asian Indians, often denied marriage licenses to Indian-white couples. As a result, Asian Indian men seeking to marry Caucasian women had to travel to states like Arizona, where such marriages were permitted. One couple figured out an imaginative way to skirt the law. They were married at sea, outside of the three-mile limit of California. According to a 1923 newspaper, "the groom was Sandar Din . . . and his bride, Berilla M. Nutter . . . both of Sutter County." After they had been refused a marriage license in two different counties, the couple went to San Francisco. There the groom "hired a launch . . . and when the boat reached the three-mile limit the captain performed the marriage ceremony and the party returned."

Many Asian Indian men married Mexican women. In northern California between 1913 and 1946, almost half of all women who were married to Asian Indian men were Mexican. In central California, 75% of the immigrants' wives were Mexican. And in southern California, where most of the Asian Indians with families lived, 92% of the wives were Mexican. "There have already been quite a few marriages between Mexican women and Hindustani men," noted an Asian Indian in California in 1923. More than half of the Mexican wives were immigrants themselves. Most of these wives were young, usually 12 to 20 years younger than their husbands. Most of these women were farm laborers who met their husbands while working. Many Punjabi-Mexican mar-

Young women practice traditional Indian dances in Massachusetts. Committed to making a future for themselves in America, people of Asian Indian descent faced the challenge of preserving their ethnic heritage while claiming their place in Western society.

riages involved sisters: One sister would marry an Asian Indian man and then introduce her sister to a friend of her husband.

Such marriages were signs that the Sikhs were planning to stay permanently in the United States, making it their new homeland. These marriages often enabled the Sikhs to buy land, because Mexican immigrants could become naturalized citizens. The land laws did not prevent the Mexican wives of Asian Indian men from owning land. Some of these men bought land in their wives' names. For example, Lohar Bupara married Teresa, a Mexican immigrant, and bought land for farming under her name. Inder Singh, a farmer in the Imperial

Valley, told an interviewer in 1924, "Two years ago I married a Mexican woman and through her I am able to secure land for farming. Your land law can't get rid of me now; I am going to stay."

The Punjabis' families in India generally did not approve of their marriages to Mexican women. "It used to be that our folks in India objected to such marriages," said Sucha Singh in 1924. He himself had not written to his family about his marriage to a Mexican woman. "I suppose others have told them about it," he said, "but I do not care even if they should be 'sour' about it."

Asian Indian–Mexican marriages had their share of cultural differences and conflicts. "My wife is inclined to be like the American women to a certain degree," explained Inder Singh. "The American woman is entirely too free; she is the boss. . . . My wife would like to boss me, but I am not disturbed by that and we get along very well." Singh had learned to take American customs in stride. At first he had been "really shocked by the freedom of the women" in America. "I have now grown accustomed to the practice of men and women going along the streets together. If I were to return to India, I believe I would carry out this practice over there." But Singh also complained that there was "entirely too much divorce here because the women were so free." Of his own wife, Singh said, "Should she at any time want to leave me I would tell her, 'The road is wide; go ahead.' "

In these Asian Indian–Mexican families, cultural traditions were often blended. Foods were exchanged—the men learned to eat tortillas instead of rotis and Mexican jalapeño peppers instead of Punjabi chili peppers. Languages were also mixed together. A Mexican wife generally understood some of her husband's native language, but their children spoke English and Spanish in the home, and Punjabi fathers learned to speak Spanish. The children were usually given Spanish first names such as Armando, José, and Rudolfo. A few of the sons had Indian names, but they went by their Spanish names or nicknames. Mexican mothers told an interviewer, "Gurbachen? Oh, you mean Bacho," and "Kishen? That's Domingo." Lohar and Teresa Bupara named their three children Sarjit, Oscar, and Anna Luisa; the oldest, Sarjit, spoke Spanish, English, and Punjabi.

Asian Indian husbands and Mexican wives generally kept their own religions. The men remained Sikhs or Muslims, and the women kept their Roman Catholic faith. Sometimes a Sikh or Muslim husband would take part in a Catholic marriage ceremony so that his wife could continue to take communion in her church. Moola Singh's wife, Susanna, said, "I'm a Catholic. . . . Well, God gives a lot of different languages . . . but I don't think so many Gods."

Children were baptized as Catholics and raised in the traditions of the Spanish culture and the Catholic church. Their godparents were usually other Punjabi-Mexican couples. The godmother helped to give religious instruction, and the godfather provided advice and presents such as bicycles and confirmation dresses.

In addition to godparents, the children also had many "uncles"—their fathers' unmarried Punjabi friends. There must have been many "uncles," for most of the Asian Indian immigrants were destined to remain bachelors. These "uncles" were often work partners of the married men and lived in the family's household. They told the children stories about the

Punjab and made them traditional Indian treats such as lemon
pickles and sweet milk desserts. On Sundays, they gave the
children money for movies and ice cream.

Many of these "uncles" were not really bachelors, for
they had wives and children in India. They were a community
of men separated from their wives. Some tried to forget their
loneliness with alcohol or prostitutes. Alcoholism was a problem that led to brawls and even murders within the Asian
Indian community.

"Quite a few of them [the immigrants] were in the
habit of drinking strong liquors, such as whiskey and brandy,
and very often got drunk," said an Asian Indian observer.
Another immigrant, working in the asparagus fields, sadly
witnessed his countrymen drinking themselves into "forget-
fulness." He saw them "drinking up their wages in order to
forget they were alive. All the old Indian bringing up was being

*A family in Lincoln,
Nebraska, in 1957.
By this time, the Asian
Indian population in the
United States had begun to
grow again after reaching a
low of 2,400 in 1940.*

swept away by a few months of inhumanly cruel work."
Alcoholism was a leading cause of death among the Punjabi
immigrants in the early period.

One reason that so many of the Punjabis felt boredom
and despair was that they had little to do during their leisure
hours. Their main pastime was talking together in what one
immigrant called "unnecessary discussion and debate, which,
however it might sharpen their wits, often led to arguments
and quarrels."

Religion, however, gave comfort and order to their
lives. Religious occasions reinforced the immigrants' sense of
their ethnic identity and helped build a feeling of Asian Indian
community in America. Muslim Asian Indians observed the
fast of Ramadan. "They fasted from moon to moon and ate
little at certain appointed hours," recalled one immigrant. A
group of Muslim Asian Indians worked as hop pickers, harvesting a plant that is used in the making of beer. Among them
was a man who had made a pilgrimage to Mecca, a city in
Saudi Arabia that is the holiest place for Muslims. This man
was the only one of the hop pickers who could read the Koran,
the Muslim holy book, in Arabic. The other workers wanted
him to read aloud to them, but they felt it would be wrong to
have him sit on the floor to read the Koran. They piled up
bales of hay about eight feet high and had him read from the
top of this pile. For hours and hours, he prayed loudly,
praising God, "O Allah, the Almighty Allah, the Compassion-
ate." After the period of fasting was over, the workers prepared for the feast. "They bought three big rams and after a
great deal of prayer and benediction, cut their throats." During their feast, the Muslims made music by beating tin cans,
and they sang all night:

Your hair is like a panther's shadow.
Your eyebrows are like the curve of a hawk's wings.

The Sikhs, too, brought their religious traditions with them into their new home in the United States. Said one immigrant, "Wherever there are 20 or 25 Sikhs, there is a temple also, which is sometimes nothing but a shack used for divine service." The temple was called a *Gurdwara* (the name means "gateway of the guru"; a guru is a teacher or spiritual guide). Each temple had a priest. Usually the priest was one of the workers in the gang who was responsible for the religious exercises and the care of the temple. Priests were elected each year and received a salary as well as room and board.

Not all of the Sikh temples were humble sheds. In Stockton, the Sikhs built an elaborate two-story temple. On the ground floor were a meeting hall and rooms for the priest's residence. Upstairs was the prayer hall where the Granth, the sacred book of the Sikh gurus, was kept on the altar. The prayer hall was decorated with rich carpets and a canopy, and pictures and texts hung on the walls. There the priest would read the scriptures twice daily. Sikhs from throughout northern California visited the Stockton Gurdwara four to six times a year, especially on major festival days. The primary purpose of this and other temples was to provide places where the immigrants could gather to worship and celebrate religious festivals, but the temples also became community centers where the Asian Indians could socialize, settle quarrels, and help newcomers.

But the temples served a dwindling Punjabi population, a community of forgotten immigrants. By 1940, accord-

*Recent newcomers to the United
States from India celebrate a
child's ninth birthday. The joys
of family life were almost
unknown to the first generation
of Asian Indian immigrants.*

ing to the U.S. census, the Asian Indian population in the
United States had dropped to 2,400, more than half of whom
lived in California. This shrinking community was made up
mostly of older people. One-third of them were over 50 years
of age, and more than half of them were over 40. In terms of
their occupations, 65% were in agriculture; only 4% were
professionals such as doctors or teachers. More than one-third
of the Asian Indian adults had not completed even one year
of schooling. Their educational level was the lowest of all the
racial and ethnic groups reported in the census.

Five years later, in 1945, an Asian Indian lecturer at
the University of Pennsylvania surveyed the Asian Indian
community in America. Dr. S. Chandrasekhar reported that
the community was "small and stable." Men who had been on
the move in search of jobs had settled down as heads of

families. Their children were becoming "Americanized," going to local public schools and speaking English. For the American-born generation, the children of the early immigrants, India was "unreal and far away." But whether they were immigrants or American-born, the Asian Indians felt isolated. They were uncertain of their place in American society and of their future in the country that was now their home. Lacking a sense of identity and growth, they hovered between two worlds, feeling neither truly American nor truly Indian. Said Chandrasekhar, "Some would like to go to India, marry, and return to their adopted land; some would like relatives in India to come here and share the American way of life." But their cultural ties to India had been "cut asunder," and "new blood" from the homeland could not be introduced.

Indian military police on duty in Egypt during World War II
(1939–45). The war opened the door to citizenship for Asian Indian
immigrants to the United States.

Chapter Six

Opening the Door of Democracy

BY THE LATE 1930S, ASIAN INDIANS IN THE UNITED States were struggling for the right to become citizens. Their numbers had dwindled, but they had not abandoned their quest for equal rights. They formed organizations such as the India Welfare League to seek civil rights and to help unemployed Asian Indian Americans. In 1941, when the United States entered World War II—which American leaders called "the war to defend democracy"—the Asian Indians' demand for equality in America was strengthened.

Under the leadership of Mubarak Ali Khan, the India Welfare League protested against discrimination and asked Congress for help. In 1939, a bill was introduced in Congress to give citizenship to all Asian Indian immigrants who had lived in the United States since 1924. The bill was attacked by the American Federation of Labor (AFL), which wanted to keep foreign laborers out of the country. A spokesman for the AFL warned Congress, "First, it will be the people who are here in our country now, the Chinese, Japanese, and Hindus, who want to be naturalized. Then they will find some other means of breaking some other little hole in the immigration law here and there or elsewhere."

Unwilling to wait for Congress to act, Khairata Ram Samras turned to the courts. In 1940, he filed a petition in the federal court of San Francisco challenging the *Thind* decision of 1923. He argued that denying citizenship to Asian Indian immigrants was a violation of the Constitution. But the congressional bill failed to pass, and Samras's challenge was rejected by the court.

A year later, in August 1941, President Franklin D. Roosevelt and Prime Minister Winston Churchill of Great Britain issued a document called the Atlantic Charter. It was a statement of democratic principles, including the right of peoples to choose their own form of government. Asian Indians realized that the Atlantic Charter gave them an opportunity to press for their rights in the United States. Mubarak Ali Khan of the India Welfare League and Sirdar Jagit Singh of the India League of America demanded two things: independence for India, which was still a colony of Great Britain, and naturalization rights for Asian Indians in the United States.

The war gave a boost to the Asian Indians' demand for fairer treatment. America's leaders saw that the United States needed India's help in the war against Japan. India was located in a position of great strategic importance, midway between Japan and Europe. The Allies feared that Japan might push its military campaign westward and try to join forces with Germany somewhere in western Asia. Many people in India were opposed to British rule in their country, and the Allies were afraid that Japan would use this opposition to create political chaos in Calcutta and other Indian cities, and then drive its military machinery across India. The United States and the other Allied nations realized that they depended upon India to block any such Japanese advance.

To win favor among the people of India, the U.S. Congress decided to listen to the complaints of Asian Indians in America. In March 1944, Congress introduced a bill that would allow immigrants from India to enter the United States and become citizens. The bill was supported by a congressman from New York, who claimed that oppressed people throughout the world looked to the United States for justice and equality. But Japanese propaganda was painting a picture of the United States as a place of prejudice and unfairness. By

"breaking down" the barriers against immigration and naturalization, the congressman argued, America could prove Japan wrong.

Four months later, Dr. S. Chandrasekhar of the University of Pennsylvania outlined another reason for Congress
to pass the bill. He wrote that the United States must fight
Nazi ideas about racial superiority. Pointing out that Germany claimed the right to oppress the other peoples of Europe
because they were "inferior," Chandrasekhar added:

> If the United States is successfully to combat such
> dangerous ideas, it can ill afford to practice racial
> discrimination in its relations with Asiatic countries.
> The immigration policy of this country now excludes
> nearly a quarter of the human race. America cannot

*Indian soldiers on
lookout duty in the
North African desert.
In addition to strengthening
Indians' demands for fairer
treatment in North America,
the war gave a boost to
their demands for
independence in India.*

Joyous Indian prisoners of war are liberated from a German prison camp near the end of the war in 1945.

afford to say that she wants the people of India to fight on her side and at the same time maintain that she will not have them among her immigrant groups.

The United States could not oppose the racism of the Nazis abroad and also practice racism at home. America had to live up to its "principle of equality," Chandrasekhar said, to keep faith with the millions of people in India who looked to America for "justice and fair play."

Two years later, in 1946, Congress acted. It permitted a limited number of new immigrants from India to enter the United States each year, and it let Asian Indians become naturalized citizens. In the 18 years that followed, 12,000 Indians entered the United States. One historian of immigration wrote that if Congress had not changed the law in 1946, the Asian Indian community in the United States might have become extinct.

Nearly 1,800 Asian Indians became U.S. citizens between 1947 and 1965. One of them was Dalip Singh Saund, who had come to America from the Punjab in 1919. Saund had become a successful farmer in California's Imperial Valley. For decades he had wanted to become a citizen. "I had married an American girl, and was the father of three American children," he explained in his autobiography. "I was making America my home. Thus it was only natural that I felt very uncomfortable not being able to become a citizen of the United States." Citizenship was more than a matter of political rights for Saund. It also let him own his land. "I saw that the bars of citizenship were shut tight against me," Saund said. "I knew if these bars were lifted I would see much wider gates of opportunity open to me, opportunity as existed for everybody else in the United States of America." After Saund became a naturalized citizen, he went on to be elected to the House of Representatives in 1956, serving for three terms. The war had opened the door of democracy to Saund and other Asian Indian Americans.

An Asian Indian family of the postwar era. Between 1945 and 1965, immigration from India increased slightly, but the total Asian Indian population in America remained small.

Chapter Seven

The Second Wave

ASIAN INDIANS HAD BECOME A DISAPPEARING MINORITY in the United States before World War II. By 1946, when the gates for Asian Indian immigration were reopened, there were only 1,500 Asian Indians in the country. Although new immigrants were admitted after 1946, only a few were allowed to enter each year. The total population of Asian Indians remained very small. In 1960, only 1% of all people of Asian descent in the United States were Indians.

In the mid-1960s, however, the history of Asian Americans entered a new phase. The civil rights movement was gaining strength in the United States, and racism was under attack. Seeking to end racism in the immigration laws, Congress passed a new Immigration Act in 1965. This law opened the door to immigration from Asia, with an annual quota of 20,000 immigrants from each country. In addition, family members of people already living in the United States were allowed to enter. The result was a massive second wave of Asian immigration. In the two decades from 1965 to 1985, four times as many Asian immigrants came to the United States as during the whole previous century. Canada reduced restrictions on immigration in 1967 with a new law that permitted more Asians to enter the country. Since the mid-1960s, Asian immigrants have been coming to North America in greater numbers than ever before, and many of these newcomers are South Asians.

"South Asian" is a term used to include people from all parts of the huge Indian subcontinent. In addition to India, the subcontinent includes Pakistan, which was part of India until India achieved its independence in 1947, and Bangladesh, which was created as an independent nation from the eastern section of Pakistan in 1971. Although the majority of the recent South Asian immigrants to North America are from India, there have been some Pakistanis and Bangladeshis as well. There have also been a few immigrants from Nepal, a country on India's northern border, and Sri Lanka, an island nation off India's south coast that was formerly called Ceylon.

This second wave of immigration has brought new life to the South Asian community in America. After the 1965 Immigration Act, when people from South Asia were able to

The Immigration Act of 1965 set off the second wave of immigration from India. Asian Indian communities across the United States grew rapidly, fueling the construction of temples such as this one in Malibu, California.

enter the United States in greater numbers, this shrinking ethnic community entered a period of explosive growth and increasing variety. By 1970, 20,000 newcomers had arrived from Pakistan alone. Half of the Pakistani immigrants were Punjabis. But unlike the Punjabi farmers who had come to America in the first wave of immigration, many of the second-wave Pakistani newcomers were highly educated professionals from the major cities.

Most of the South Asian immigrants who have arrived in the United States since 1965 are from India. The number of Asian Indians in the United States has climbed steeply, from 10,000 in 1965 to 800,000 in 1990. Asian Indians were once only a tiny fraction of the total Asian American population, but by 1985, they represented 10% of all Asians in the United States. Asian Indians are no longer a tiny minority isolated in the farming valleys of California. They have become very visible, especially in the northeastern states. More than one-third of all Asian Indians in the United States live in the Northeast; 18% of them live in New York alone. A section of Indian restaurants and stores on New York City's East Sixth Street has come to be known as "Little India."

These new immigrants from India are very different from those of the first wave. The first-wave immigrants were almost all men, but the second wave of immigration has been equally divided between men and women. Unlike the first-wave immigrants, the recent newcomers have come to America not as temporary workers but as settlers, with every intention of staying. Many of them have shown their determination to become part of America by applying for citizenship. By 1980, more than half of the Asian Indians who had entered the United States had become naturalized citizens.

Many of the first-wave immigrants had little or no education and spoke English poorly, if at all. But the second-wave immigrants generally speak English and are educated. In the decade after 1965, the immigrants came mostly from the professional class, which included doctors, teachers, and engineers. Said one of these newcomers, "The first Indian immigrants and the post-1965 Indian immigrants are two separate worlds. It is a class thing. They came from the farming, the lower class. We came from the educated middle class. We spoke English. We went to college. We were already assimilated in India, before we came here." Indians from the professional class have continued to arrive in North America, but in the late 1970s and early 1980s, the stream of immigration widened somewhat as the relatives of the earlier professional immigrants began to arrive. Some of these newcomers were less prosperous and well-educated than their fellow immigrants in the professions. Instead of entering law, medicine, or teaching, many of them turned to business. Beginning around 1980, North America saw the arrival of many Asian Indians who became self-employed and opened their own small businesses; some of these businesses, such as Indian restaurants and clothing shops, serve the needs of the growing ethnic community.

The immigrants of the early 20th century and those of recent years have had one important thing in common: their reason for coming to America. Like those who crossed the Pacific in the first wave of immigration, the second-wave immigrants have come mainly for economic reasons. By the 1960s, professionals in India found that their job prospects were severely limited. The number of people educated for the professions far exceeded the number of jobs available for

them. Hundreds of thousands of Indians with college degrees were unable to find employment. Unemployment was particularly serious for engineers and physicians. In 1970, for example, there were 20,000 unemployed doctors in India; four years later, the country had a "surplus" of 100,000 engineers.

Most of the second-wave Asian Indians have found that economic opportunities in North America are much better than those in their home country. Unlike some other newcomers from Asia, Asian Indians have not found themselves crowded into service jobs, such as restaurant work. In

An Asian Indian cultural festival in New Jersey. The recent immigrants face many conflicts between American and Indian customs, but religious and cultural traditions provide strong bonds of unity among Asian Indians.

the late 1980s, Asian Indians had a lower percentage of people working in service jobs than any other Asian American ethnic group. They also had the highest percentage employed as managers and professionals; nearly half of all working Asian Indian Americans fell into this category, with 25,000 Asian Indian physicians and dentists, 40,000 engineers, 20,000 scientists, and 2,000 professionals in fields such as law and banking.

Yet some Asian Indian professionals have changed their occupations after arriving in North America. Rather than working in the fields of their training, some college-educated immigrants can be found operating travel agencies, clothing shops, and luncheonettes featuring pizza, Greek dishes, or Indian "fast food" such as curry. Some operate newsstands in the subways of New York City. Newsstand owner Bawnesh Kapoor explains the advantages of his job: "You don't need a lot of capital to start. You don't have inventory problems because you normally turn over your entire inventory in a week. You don't have accounts receivable problems. You don't have to worry about changes in fashion." Asian Indians have also been investing in the motel business. More than one-quarter of the hotels and motels in the United States are owned by Asian Indians.

While many of these people have become self-employed entrepreneurs by choice, others have found themselves pushed into self-employment by discrimination. Asian Indian technicians and engineers, for example, complain about what has been called the "glass ceiling"—a point where they can see the higher-paying management jobs but cannot get into them. "The only jobs we could get were based on merit," explained Kumar Patel, head of the material science division

of AT&T. "That is why you find most [Asian Indian] professionals in technical rather than administrative or managerial
positions." Similarly, an Asian Indian engineer who had
worked for Kaiser for some 20 years told a friend, "They
[management] never even give you [Asian Indians] an executive position in the company. You can only go up so high and
no more." Frustrated by limited opportunities to advance in
their careers, many Asian Indian professionals have turned to
opening their own businesses.

In communities across the land, Asian Indian Americans are making their presence felt. In Philadelphia, where
25,000 of them had settled by the late 1980s, scores of
restaurants, print shops, car dealerships, and clothing and
jewelry shops owned by Asian Indians contribute to the city's
economy. Asian Indian businesspeople in the community
range from a millionaire dealer in used luxury cars to an
immigrant from a farming family in the Punjab who works
for 16 hours each day at his food stand in the city's university
district. The Asian Indian community in Rochester, New
York, numbers more than 500 families and includes a high
number of doctors, university professors, and scientists. New
York City, where the Asian Indian population skyrocketed
from 6,000 in 1970 to more than 94,000 in 1990, has one
of the largest Hindu temples in North America.

Asian Indian Americans have been trying to define
who they are in their adopted society. In 1975, the issue of
Asian Indian identity was raised by the U.S. government's
Census Bureau, which examined the question of whether Asian
Indians belonged to a "minority group." A government offi-
cial decided that they did not, stating that persons of Asian
Indian descent "are regarded as white." Some Asian Indians

agreed with this view. Among them were the leaders of the Chicago-based India League of America. The India League argued that it would be a mistake for their group to claim minority group status. According to the League, Asian Indians in America were not truly disadvantaged, and other Americans might turn against them if they appeared to benefit from programs, such as Equal Employment Opportunity, that were intended to help the victims of discrimination.

But many other Asian Indians believed that they should be considered a minority group. The Association of Indians in America pointed out that Asian Indians, like African Americans and other Asian groups, were discrimi-

Asian Indian parents often try to raise their children in the traditional Indian manner, but young people increasingly feel the pull of Western ways.

nated against because of their skin color. In a statement to the United States Civil Rights Commission in 1975, the Association declared: "The language of the Civil Rights Act clearly intends to protect those individuals who might be disadvantaged on the basis of appearance. It is undeniable that Indians are different in appearance; they are equally dark-skinned as other non-white individuals and are, therefore, subject to the same prejudices." The Association concluded that Asian Indians were "disadvantaged for reasons of racial discrimination."

In 1976, leaders of the Association took part in a government-sponsored meeting to discuss the ethnic categories that would be used in the 1980 national census. The meeting included representatives from the Pacific Islander, Chinese, Japanese, Filipino, and Korean communities as well as the Asian Indians. They decided that Asian Indians should be recognized as a distinct group, and the Census Bureau agreed to change the category to which immigrants from India and their descendants belonged. Instead of being included in the "white/Caucasian" group, they would be counted as "Asian Indian."

Asian Indians are proud of their ethnic heritage, yet they also want to be identified as Americans. Hamida Chopra explained it this way. She came to the United States after 1965 to join her student husband, thinking her stay in America would be only temporary. But 23 years later, she said, "America is my home." Although she chose not to become a U.S. citizen, she thinks of herself as an American. But she is also Indian. She speaks only Urdu in her home and has taught her daughter the language and culture of their ancestral land. She always wears Indian clothing, which on formal occasions means the distinctive sari—a long piece of cloth worn so that one end forms a floor-length skirt and the other is draped over the shoulder. When she first arrived, people looked at her as a foreigner, Chopra recalled. "But now these days," she noted smiling, "they look at me and have no curiosity. American society is open, able to absorb differences in cultures and dress. I feel that the definition of what is 'American' has become broader."

The definition of "American" *is* becoming broader and more multicultural. At the same time, however, a few people, feeling threatened by the growing diversity that they see around them in streets, stores, and schools, have lashed out in hate crimes against people whose ethnic backgrounds are different from theirs. In recent years, Asian Indians have been among the victims of violence fueled by prejudice.

Violence broke out in 1987 in Jersey City, New Jersey, where about 15,000 Asian Indians were living. In a series of incidents, people of Asian Indian descent were harassed by teenagers, many of whom were Puerto Ricans. Some of the Asian Indians suffered only verbal abuse, shouts of "Hindu! Hindu!" and other taunts and insults. Other victims were slapped or pelted with eggs, stones, and empty soda cans. Attackers threw stones at the houses of some Asian Indian families, and Asian Indian places of worship were vandalized. Tragically, the violence did not stop there. A man of mixed Indian and Iranian descent was beaten so severely that he died; another man, an Asian Indian immigrant, was beaten into unconsciousness on a city street.

In the wake of these events, a local newspaper printed an anonymous letter that was said to be from a racist group called the Dotbusters—a reference to the small dot called the *bindi* that some Asian Indian women wear on their foreheads for religious reasons. The Dotbusters said, "We will go to any extreme to get Indians to move out of Jersey City," and threatened more violence against people of Asian Indian descent. The writer of the letter claimed that the Dotbusters targeted their victims by looking for Asian Indian names in the phone book.

The Asian Indian community reacted with fear and outrage, calling for increased investigation of racial crimes and for better police protection. Five hundred Asian Indians marched through Jersey City to urge police action with the slogan "We want justice!" Young men formed community watch groups to patrol their streets and neighborhoods. Concern spread far outside Jersey City. Asian Indians around the United States discussed the troubling issue of anti-Indian prejudice and racial crime, both in local meetings and in the pages of *India West* and *India Abroad*, newspapers that serve Asian Indians in America. Asian Indians knew that the problem was not confined to New Jersey; they had suffered harassment and vandalism in Chicago, Long Island, New York City, and elsewhere. In December 1987, a few months after the beatings in Jersey City, Asian Indian community leaders from all over the country attended a national meeting and formed an organization to combat anti-Indian racism and racial violence through public demonstrations and legal and political action.

Much of the violence against Asian Indians has been economic in origin. In Jersey City, where some of the attackers were members of the large Puerto Rican immigrant community, the outbreak showed the resentment of one group of immigrants against another that seemed to be outdoing them in jobs and income. Many of the area's factories and large industries have closed, and unemployment is high, especially among unskilled and semiskilled laborers. Asian Indians have opened shops, restaurants, and other businesses in and around Jersey City, but because of their tradition of shared family enterprise, their employees are often relatives, which has contributed to the frustration of non-Indians who cannot find jobs. Puerto Rican immigrants, some of whom lack English-language skills, are especially hard hit by the shortage of jobs; if they cannot speak English, they will be passed over for service jobs that require them to deal with the public.

Hard times and economic pressures have created frustration and hostility toward those who are seen as different, as outsiders and strangers. Racial and ethnic crimes are rooted in economic problems of unemployment, boarded-up factories, and lack of educational opportunities that can prepare people for jobs. In addition, racial antagonisms reflect the ways different groups view one another through negative stereotypes. In the late 1980s, some young members of the Asian Indian community recognized the need for multicultural education to combat this ignorance. After the outbreak of ethnic violence in Jersey City, Asian Indian students at New York City's Columbia University formed a group called Indian Youth Against Racism (IYAR). They were concerned about the anti-Indian hostility in New Jersey and elsewhere, but, as one of the founders said, "We also wanted to . . . align ourselves with other groups which also suffer from racism—blacks, Hispanics, and even some of the groups which were minorities a few decades ago."

Members of IYAR have worked to reduce racism in several ways. Some of their actions were political; for example, they lobbied for the passage of a New Jersey law that set new, harsher penalties for crimes that have an element of racism. Other activities were educational in nature. IYAR members helped write a pamphlet for teachers that outlined some key aspects of Indian culture, hoping to bring to non-Indians a greater understanding of customs that are shaped by Indian tradition and religion.

IYAR members felt that the best way to destroy racial myths and stereotypes was to educate young people. In discussions that followed the Jersey City incidents, IYAR came up with the idea of confronting racism in the schools. "They were convinced that racism should be fought from the earliest stage, and while it might not be easy to change the racial attitude of the adults, it was worth trying to do so with young students," explained an educator who worked with IYAR to develop a teaching project for a Jersey City high school. The project brought together several dozen students of different races for two weeks, during which racial stereotypes were brought into the open and replaced with facts and shared experiences.

Similar educational projects are now being used to counteract racial tension in many school systems. They are promoting communication among ethnic groups—something that is vital to a tolerant, multicultural society. As a young American-born Asian Indian woman said, "We are here with whites, blacks, Jews, Hispanics, and we have to learn to live together and respect each other's hopes, desires, and ambitions."

People of Indian descent have not always been clearly recognized as Asian Americans. Because the physical appearance and ethnic background of most Indians are different from those of Chinese, Japanese, and Koreans, Asian Indians have sometimes overlooked their kinship with these peoples. In the 1920s, for example, immigrants from India were certain that they possessed citizenship rights in the United States, even though Japanese immigrants had just been turned down in their request for such rights. Regarding themselves as Caucasians rather than Asians, Asian Indians confidently applied for citizenship. But the U.S. Supreme Court rejected the Indians' plea in the *Thind* case, just as it had rejected the Japanese in the *Ozawa* case. The newcomers from India found that they had more in common with their Asian brethren than they had realized.

In recent years, too, Asian Indians have had to take a fresh look at their place in the history of immigration and discrimination. For example, in the 1980s the city of San Francisco passed a law that set aside a certain share of the contracts through which the city purchased labor, services, and supplies. These contracts were to be given to minority businesses. Yet in 1989, San Francisco ruled that Asian Indians were not a minority under the terms of the program; Asian Indian contractors, therefore, could not receive the reserved contracts. In effect, the city was claiming that Asian Indians had not been discriminated against as a minority.

The Asian Indian Association of America (AIAA) fought the city's decision, pointing out that people from India—like immigrants from China, Japan, and Korea—had suffered from anti-Asian discrimination since they first arrived in the United States at the beginning of the 20th century. Just like members of other Asian immigrant groups, they had been forbidden to become citizens, to own land, or to intermarry freely with whites. They were driven out of their homes by angry crowds chanting "Whites only." And discrimination was not merely a thing of the past. Recent incidents showed that Asian Indians, like other new immigrants from Asia, still had to overcome some racial barriers. San Francisco reversed its decision, granting minority status to Asian Indian contractors, and Asian Indian Americans moved a step closer to claiming their place not just in U.S. society as a whole but within the Asian American community as well.

An emblem of India in the West, the Malibu temple represents the traditions and beliefs at the core of Indian culture. Young Asian Indian Americans, however, feel the need to define themselves as both Indian and American—a process that is sometimes painful.

ALL IMMIGRANT GROUPS HAVE FACED THE QUESTION OF whether they should cling to their cultural roots or try to become "American" as quickly as possible. Assimilation—blending into the larger society—has been more difficult for Asian immigrants than for European ones, for Asians can be identified by their physical appearance even when their clothing, speech, and actions have been completely Americanized. Those Asians who choose to follow traditional customs stand out even more readily. The earliest Asian Indian immigrants to North America were singled out as "strangers" because of their turbans. Today, as the Dotbusters case in New Jersey shows, the customs of Asian Indian Americans continue to make them vulnerable to racism.

Following the Dotbusters episode, Asian Indian newspapers in the United States were full of letters about the wisdom of keeping alive such traditions as the bindi, the sari, and the turban. One writer recommended that Asian Indian women stop wearing their traditional dress because it reinforced the image of Asian Indians as "foreigners" and made the women targets of racial attacks. Not all readers agreed. Another member of the community replied indignantly, "I strongly urge all Indians to take pride in our rich and glorious culture. Let not the racist and bigoted actions of a few undermine our ethnic and nationalistic pride." In 1991, an Asian Indian historian at Queens College in New York noted, "The tension is increasing between maintaining Indian traditions and adapting to American society. This is a society very much at a crossroads."

Many Asian Indians insist on their right to claim both identities. For example, Dr. S. Patel said, "I am, I know, both Indian and American." When she arrived in the United States in 1967, she planned to remain for only five years. "Mine was an arranged marriage," she explained. "My husband was studying in the United States and I came here to be with him. But then my son was born. Meanwhile I also passed my examination for my medical license and did my internship. So one thing led to another. And five years extended into ten years. And we found ourselves staying permanently."

Still, Patel misses her homeland. She and her husband visit India every three years, taking their children with them. "When my husband and I pass away, I don't think my children will be visiting India," she remarked. "My children will probably give their children American names. I would like my son to marry an Indian, but I would let him make his own choice." She is concerned about divorce, however. "In an Indian marriage there is no divorce. Yes, marriage does have its ups and downs. But divorce is out of the question in Indian culture. So that is what I would worry about if my son did not marry an Indian woman."

In the years immediately after 1965, Patel observed, the newly arrived immigrants were too busy trying to survive to have time to think about their community or ethnicity. She added, "But now we are established professionally, and we have time to think about our future in America." For her, ethnic identity is political as well as personal. "Indians have to organize to be visible and to have influence," she said. "I am not political. I am too busy being a mother and working. But I am concerned about the tightening of laws about doctors from foreign countries practicing here. It would make it more difficult for doctors from India to come here. So we as Indians have to be concerned."

Like almost all of the second-wave Asian Indians, Patel has made America her home. But she admitted in a moment of reflection, "Now that I think about it I sometimes would like to move back to India. Why? Because there is too much individualism here in America. I am getting old and I am afraid my children will grow up and will not be near me. In India, children take care of their parents. This doesn't happen in this country. So there is a price to be paid for coming here. The family isn't as close here."

One area in which second-generation Asian Indian Americans tend to differ from their parents is in their sense of attachment to the homeland. Their parents maintain a passionate interest in events within India, eagerly snapping up copies of Indian newspapers and debating India's political and social issues at great length. But although many in the younger generation visit India and maintain close ties with their relatives there, most young Asian Indian Americans are less interested in events in India than in their future in America. A member of the New York–based group Indian Youth Against Racism explained, "Most of us have been born here, or were brought up in this country for the most part. Of course, we are interested in what is happening [in India] but our primary concern is the Indian community in this country."

The children of immigrants, who have grown up in two different worlds, face the special challenge of searching for their identity. Asian Indian children are no exception. At times they feel confused, not knowing whether to think of themselves as Indians or as Americans. At home, Indian values and customs remain strong—especially the tradition of un-questioning obedience to one's father. Yet at school and in the larger world, young people feel the pull of American culture and its values, which include questioning authority and making one's own decisions. The result is frequent disagreement over how much freedom young Asian Indians should have.

"Indian parents maintain a much higher level of discipline in their homes," wrote a young man in an essay for *India West.* "Indian children have more rules thrust upon them, more orders to follow, higher expectations about their behavior. While the children are young, these expectations are bearable, though they are difficult to understand. But when we reach our teenage years, when our peers are setting their own curfews, making their own decisions, this extra discipline seems dictatorial and burdensome."

Much of the conflict between old and new revolves around family life, the roles of women and children, and marriage—areas that in Indian culture are closely governed by tradition. Many young people chafe at the rules imposed by their parents, who seem much stricter than other American parents. One boy recalled his anger over an incident that occurred when he went to a concert with his friends. All of them came home at the same time, but the Asian Indian boy was the only one who got into trouble—his parents thought that he had been out too late. An Asian Indian American lawyer in Rochester, New York, recalled, "I used to fume and cry when my parents would not allow me to stay out with my friends." Then he added, "But now that I have two sons, I probably will be the same with them."

A worried 35-year-old immigrant parent spoke of the growing influence of American culture on his daughters, who were five and nine years old. "They see too much openness of

women, like on the beach when they are half naked," he said. "It's hard, because our children are picking up Western values, but I still want them to look to me for Indian guidance." He and his wife worked to keep their Indian heritage alive, playing Indian records and speaking their native language at home. Yet his small daughters, who already preferred Western-style clothes and music, had begun to move away from their Indian roots.

Perhaps the single most troublesome issue between parents and children in Asian Indian American families has been dating. In traditional Indian culture, dating is unheard of; boys and girls have very little contact with one another

A ceremony in a Pittsburgh, Pennsylvania, temple. No longer limited to the West Coast or to the largest cities, Asian Indians are making their presence felt throughout multicultural America.

before marriage, which is arranged by their parents. Dating is completely foreign to traditional Indian ideas about the proper relationship between the sexes. Yet dating is almost universal among young people in America. Many Asian Indian parents are willing to see their children adopt some American pastimes but draw the line at dating. Others permit sons to date, but not daughters; still others allow their children to date only other Asian Indians. Some teenagers accept these restrictions, even if they do so unhappily. Others, however, feel that the rules that applied in India have little place in the modern United States, and they often defy their parents.

"Growing up in two cultures is a great challenge, yes, but not a problem," wrote the young Asian Indian man who had argued with his parents about coming home late from the concert. "It is a difficult experience, but not one without its benefits. Growing up in two cultures broadens our horizons; it allows us to experience the best of the east and the best of the west. . . . I, for one, feel that I am a better person for being both Indian and American." His remarks were echoed by a 20-year-old medical student in New York, whose statement could apply to all children of immigrants, including Japanese American, Hispanic American, or Irish American as well as Asian Indian American: "There are youngsters who feel pulled by two cultures. It is important to glean the best of both worlds. You can do it."

Old and new customs conflict with one another in the realm of marriage. Among traditional Indians, marriages are arranged by families and are based upon such things as the social status and the wealth of the bride's or groom's family. In North America, on the other hand, marriage is regarded as a personal choice based on love. Some Asian Indian families, especially those in which the children were born or grew up in the United States, have moved toward the American concept of marriage. They understand that young people expect greater independence in choosing their partners. Although family members' opinions may still have greater weight than is the case in mainstream American society, children in these families generally have considerable freedom of choice. Some of them marry non-Indians.

Other families, however, take a more traditional approach to marriage. This is especially true of families who arrived in the United States with youngsters who were already past early childhood. Indian values are more firmly fixed in such families, and many marriages are still arranged by parents. Lacking the network of marriage advisers, relatives, and family friends who act as matchmakers in India, Asian Indians in North America may turn to the newspapers to seek husbands or wives for their children. *India West* and *India Abroad* contain marriage advertisements. Such an ad might begin "Matrimonial alliance sought for handsome Punjabi, 40, well-settled businessman" or "Doctor brother invites correspondence for good-looking, home-loving, charming sister, 32, immigrant." But mixed in among these ads placed by family members are ads placed by people seeking their own mates. These ads are no different from the personal ads that people of all ethnic backgrounds sometimes use to meet possible partners. They are a sign that young Asian Indian Americans are beginning to take marriage matters into their own hands. As more sons and daughters of Asian Indian immigrants rebel against the notion of arranged marriages, the Indian community's newspapers, temples, and social centers are likely to see an increase in young people doing their own matchmaking. Intermarriage with non-Indians will probably increase as well.

Asian Indians face the problems of being a minority within American society, but Asian Indian women face a double challenge, for they are a minority within a minority. About half of all Asian Indian immigrant women in the United States work outside the home. These women are represented in high-level jobs in industry, science, education, law, and medicine—although they hold far fewer such jobs than men do. Nevertheless, in the majority of Asian Indian households, women are also expected to do all the housework, even if they work full-time. The traditions of Asian Indian culture say that the home is the woman's responsibility, just as men are expected to make all important decisions, such as where to live or how to educate the children. But as women everywhere challenge these limits and demand equal rights, Asian Indian women are beginning to change their roles in the family, the workplace, and the community. They have formed a number of organizations to aid newly arriving immigrant women, to express their concerns to politicians and educators, and to carry out community projects. These groups include the South Asian Women's Network in Los Angeles, the South Asia Community Center in Montreal, and the Association of Asian Indian Women in America in New York.

The Asian Indian population in America began growing dramatically since 1965, but it is still a very small part of the total U.S. population. It was even smaller in 1973, when Latha Kumar's family moved to a small southern town. Her experiences growing up in that community show that it is awkward to be a "stranger" in town, even when the townsfolk are friendly. Kumar's family was only the second Indian family in that community; she and her brother were the first two Asian Indian students to graduate from the local high school. In an article in *India Abroad*, she recalled:

> I went to school with kids who could and did ask questions that I found difficult to answer. Being an Indian put me in a special position: to them I was that "Indian girl with the pretty hair." Try being 10 years old and answer these questions:
> Why does your mom wear a dot on her forehead?
> Why does your mom wear that long piece of cloth?
> Why doesn't your family eat meat?
> Did you ever ride an elephant?
> Needless to say, some of these questions were really hard to answer, especially to a kid.

Kumar found that most of her schoolmates knew little about India and Indian people. To some of them, she might as well have been "from another planet." She was often mistaken for a Native American Indian. "One kid begged me to do a rain dance," she said. "Another thought I was an Apache."

She experienced another problem that plagues many ethnic children who are treated as spokespeople for their parents' homelands:

> All of my teachers also expected me to be a sort of "ambassador from India," even though I grew up here. That meant that I should know everything about India, including Hinduism, and explain it to the whole class, every time the topic ever came up. The truth was

I knew less about certain aspects of it than my teachers.

The teenage years were particularly difficult for Kumar. Other girls her age began dating, but her family followed Indian tradition, which meant that she could not date. "That was when being different really hurt," she said. She "hated being Indian" because there were no other kids in her situation, "no one that I could identify with."

Latha Kumar was born in the United States, but the tension between Indian and American ways is even stronger in the lives of women who come to America from traditional South Asian cultures. The mixture of cultures in immigrants' lives is captured in the award-winning fiction of Bharati Mukherjee, who was born in Calcutta, India. Mukherjee lived in Canada from 1966 until 1980, when she came to the United States to write and teach. Many of the characters in her stories and novels are immigrants who have come to Canada or the United States. Some of them have been deeply affected by racism.

Ratna, the heroine of the story "The World According to Hsu," is a half-Indian woman who lives in Montreal. Her husband tries to convince her that they should move to Toronto, but she fears that she would encounter greater racism there. Ratna and her husband visit a strife-torn island off the coast of Africa, where the influences of black African, Arab, Indian, and European cultures swirl and clash. Ratna meditates on the prejudice that causes the people of Toronto to refer to all South Asians as "Pakis," an insulting term for Pakistanis. She listens to news bulletins from Toronto: a Bengali woman is beaten in the street; a Punjabi boy is run down by a car bearing the bumper sticker "Keep Canada Green. Paint a Paki." By the end of the story, she realizes that on the island, for all its cultural confusion, she feels more comfortable and alive than she felt in Canada. The island is the birthplace of a new kind of world citizen, one who belongs to all countries and to no country. It is a "collection of Indians and Europeans babbling in English and remembered dialects." The story ends: "No matter where she lived, she would never feel so at home again."

In Mukherjee's story "A Father," an Asian Indian family in Detroit deals with the consequences of a young

Dalip Singh Saund with President John F. Kennedy. Saund was the only South Asian ever elected to the U.S. House of Representatives, serving from 1956 to 1962.

107

Dr. S. Chandrasekhar
of the University of Chicago,
who won the Nobel Prize
in 1983 for his pioneering
work on the structure
and evolution of stars.

woman's sexuality. When Babli, the daughter, becomes pregnant, her father wrestles with his feelings of shame and outrage. "Girls like Babli were caught between rules," he tells himself—they were too smart and sophisticated for India, but not tough and smart enough for "sex-crazy places like Detroit." In "A Wife's Story," an Asian Indian woman in New York reacts with anger and dignity when characters in a play insult South Asian women. Later, she imagines herself writing to director Steven Spielberg, who portrayed India and Indians in crude stereotypes in his movie *Indiana Jones and the Temple of Doom,* to "tell him that Indians don't eat monkey brains." She reflects on how immigrants are treated in America: "First, you don't exist. Then you're invisible. Then you're funny. Then you're disgusting."

Yet America offers opportunities as well as insults. In the story "Jasmine," the heroine is a young Asian Indian woman, born on the Caribbean island of Trinidad, who comes to Michigan by way of Canada as an illegal immigrant, with "no visa, no papers, and no birth certificate." As Mukherjee says, Jasmine was "nothing other than what she wanted to invent and tell. She was a girl rushing wildly into the future."

Tara Bannerjee, the heroine of Mukherjee's novel *The Tiger's Daughter*, comes from Calcutta to attend college in the United States, marries, and then returns to India after seven years in America. In the first pages of the book, Tara sees America through Asian eyes; she is surprised and shaken by scenes of poverty and violence. After her marriage, when she moves to New York with her husband, she views the city as alien and frightening. "New York was certainly extraordinary," writes Mukherjee, "and it had driven her to despair. On days she had thought she could not possibly survive, she had shaken out all her silk scarves, ironed them and hung them to make the apartment more 'Indian.' She had curried hamburger desperately till David's stomach had protested."

Yet when Tara revisits Calcutta, she is made uncomfortably aware of a side of India that she had not recognized during her privileged girlhood in a wealthy family. She witnesses poverty, violence, and unrest. At times she feels like an alien visitor in her homeland. India is changing; Calcutta is caught up in a whirlwind of social and political unrest. Tara too has changed. She is no longer just like the Indian women who are her friends and relatives. She cannot rid herself of the ideas and values she has acquired in America. Like thousands of real-life immigrants in New York, Toronto, and California, Tara has become something new: an Asian Indian American.

What happened to Tara had also happened to other Asian Indians who began coming to America in the early 20th century and who arrived in increasing numbers after 1965. Whether they came initially thinking they would stay only temporarily, or whether they came as settlers seeking a new home, all of them found themselves changed by America as they built Sikh temples in the valleys of California, farmed the new land, practiced medicine, operated small businesses, and raised their children. But although Tara and her fellow Asian Indian Americans have been changed by their experiences in the West, in the process they have also been changing America, making its society richer and more multicultural.

Chronology

1903–6	Workers from India begin emigrating to Canada and the United States.
1907	White mobs drive Asian Indian workers out of Bellingham and Everett, Washington.
1914	Sikhs aboard the *Komagata Maru* attempt to enter Canada and are forcibly turned away.
1917	The U.S. Congress bars entry of Asian Indians.
1923	In the *Thind case,* the U.S. Supreme Court rules that Asian Indians cannot become U.S. citizens.
1924	The U.S. Congress bans immigration from Asia.
1939–45	Britain, the United States, and their allies need India's support during World War II.
1946	The United States allows limited immigration from India and permits Indian immigrants to become naturalized U.S. citizens.
1947	India receives independence from Great Britain; the independent nation of Pakistan is created from the Muslim districts of India.
1952	Canada allows 250 immigrants to enter each year from India and Pakistan.

1965   The United States passes a new immigration law that opens the door for a second wave of Asian immigrants, including many from India and Pakistan.

1967   Canada passes a new immigration law that admits Asian Indians on equal terms with immigrants from other countries.

Further Reading

Bagai, Leona B. *The East Indians and the Pakistanis in America.* Minneapolis: Lerner, 1972.

Buchighani, Norman, and Doreen M. Indra. *Continuous Journey: A Social History of South Asians in Canada.* Toronto: McClelland and Stewart, 1985.

Chadney, James S. *The Sikhs of Vancouver.* New York: AMS Press, 1984.

Chandrasekhar, S., ed. *From India to America.* La Jolla, CA: Population Review, 1984.

———. *From India to Canada.* La Jolla, CA: Population Review, 1986.

Gordon, Susan. *Asian Indians.* New York: Franklin Watts, 1990.

Jensen, Joan M. *Passage from India: Asian Indian Immigrants in North America.* New Haven, CT: Yale University Press, 1988.

Leonard, Karen. *California's Punjabi Mexican Americans.* Philadelphia: Temple University Press, 1983.

Melendy, H. Brett. *Asians in America: Filipinos, Koreans, and East Indians.* Boston: Twayne, 1977.

Mukherjee, Bharati. *Darkness.* New York: Fawcett Crest, 1985.

————. *The Middleman and Other Stories.* New York: Fawcett Crest, 1988.

————. *The Tiger's Daughter.* New York: Fawcett Crest, 1971.

————. *Wife.* Boston: Houghton Mifflin, 1975.

Saund, D. S. *Congressman from India.* New York: Dutton, 1960.

Index

RONALD TAKAKI, the son of immigrant plantation laborers from Japan, graduated from the College of Wooster, Ohio, and earned his Ph.D. in history from the University of California at Berkeley, where he has served both as the chairperson and the graduate adviser of the Ethnic Studies program. Professor Takaki has lectured widely on issues relating to ethnic studies and multiculturalism in the United States, Japan, and the former Soviet Union and has won several important awards for his teaching efforts. He is the author of six books, including the highly acclaimed *Strangers from a Different Shore: A History of Asian Americans,* and the recently published *A Different Mirror: A History of Multicultural America.*

REBECCA STEFOFF is a writer and editor who has published more than 50 nonfiction books for young adults. Many of her books deal with geography and exploration, including the three-volume set *Extraordinary Explorers,* recently published by Oxford University Press. Stefoff also takes an active interest in environmental issues. She served as editorial director for two Chelsea House series—*Peoples and Places of the World* and *Let's Discover Canada.* Stefoff studied English at the University of Pennsylvania, where she taught for three years. She lives in Portland, Oregon.